Values, Aspiration and Professional Education

A Predictive Analysis among Undergraduate Students

Values, Aspiration and Professional Education

A Predictive Analysis among Undergraduate Students

Dr Afzalur Rahman

KALPAZ

First Published, 2018

Published by

Kalpaz Publications
C-30, Satyawati Nagar,
Delhi – 110052
E-mail: kalpaz@hotmail.com
Ph.: 9212142040

Printed at: G. Print Process, Delhi

Cataloging in Publication Data—DK
Courtesy: D.K. Agencies (P) Ltd. <docinfo@dkagencies.com>

Rahman, Afzalur (Md. Afzalur), author.
Values, aspiration and professional education : a predictive analysis among undergraduate students / Dr Afzalur Rahman.
pages cm
"Original title of the Ph. D. dissertation: Value dimensions of undergraduate students of professional courses in relation to their level of aspiration."
Includes bibliographical references.
ISBN 9789386397386 (HB)

1. Values—Study and teaching (Higher)—India. 2. Professional education—India. 3. Level of aspiration—India. 4. Undergraduates—India—Psychology. I. Title.

LCC BF778.R34 2018 | DDC 121.8 23

Contents

Foreword

Values are set of principles or standards of behaviour, they are regarded desirable, important and held in high esteem by a particular society in which a person lives, and the failure to hold them will result in blame, criticism or condemnation. Values are those standards or codes of conduct, which are conditioned by one's cultural tenets guided by conscience, according to which one is supposed to conduct himself and shape his life pattern by integrating his belief, ideas and attitudes with a view to realise the cherished ideals and aims of life. Thus, values give meaning and strength to a person's character by occupying a central place in our life. Vales reflect one's personal attitudes and judgements, one's decisions and choices, one's behaviour and relationships, one's dreams and vision. They influence our thought, feelings and dreams.

Indian society has offered great value system to human kind. According to Indian philosophers, knowledge has two functions- (i) Theoretical-revealing the existence of some object (artha parichitti) and (ii) Practical-helping in fulfilment of a purpose in life (phala prapti). The first one is known as 'fact' and the other as 'value'. Both are interrelated because knowledge of fact leads to pursuit of a value. Besides the four values namely- Dharma (virtue), Artha (wealth), Kama (pleasure) and Moksha (liberation), the Indian philosophical system also holds other values like truth and goodness. When combined with beauty, they become philosophical trio 'Satyam', 'Shivam' and 'Sundaram'- the trinity of values. 'Ahimsha' is the latest addition to Indian value system. Such a rich Indian values have always taught peaceful coexistence of multiple sections of the people.

The human society of 21st century is facing a tremendous value crisis. There is devaluation of values in various aspects of life, relating to political, social, philosophical, economic, commercial, educational, cultural and administrative and so many other fields. Truthfulness, tolerance, honesty and integrity, co-operation, mutual love and affection etc., which are necessary for smooth running of a society, unfortunately have almost vanished. The conflict between traditional and modernity may be considered as one of the major factors of value crisis in Indian society. People began to think that the old Indian values are outdated and are slowly unlearnt and no new values that are worthwhile, are learnt. For the present day generation, the only well known value of success in life is 'success at any cost and by any means', that resulted in personal greed, selfishness, meanness, indifference to others etc. Modern age of science and technology has created certain evils like industrialisation, and consequent urbanisation of life has given rise to a kind of commercial outlook to life in all its manifestations. All these factors have resulted in value crisis.

The system of education, which is viewed as the treasure house and transmission of ethics and values, seems to be failed today in its very purpose. The education is day by day becoming more materialistic and stress has been mainly given on earning bread and butter. As a result most of our educated people are running after money, power and comforts without caring for any moral values. Considering the deficiency on the part of present education system, stress is given on the role of value education and also on the role of universities as the facilitator of values. What is expected from the universities is that they should cultivate the basic values to the students. Thus, it is imperative need in the present context that the whole education system should be reconstructed so as to include value education as an implicit aspect of the same. If we wish to save our society from total collapse and improve the quality of life, we have to reinstate and inculcate desirable values in the growing minds.

I am glad that Afzalur Rahman, in this book entitled 'Values, Aspiration and Professional Education' has done and presented an extensive work in the field of value education. The variables discussed in the book namely 'Values', 'Level of Aspiration' and 'Professional Education' are interrelated and are very relevant in the present context, since level of aspiration affects the value system of the professionals.

Sometimes high level of aspiration forces the individual to change their value pattern in specific situation. The personality or self-concept becomes concrete by the time the students enters the professional course after plus two stage. They become independent in deciding their vocational choices and to grow in that profession progressively. Therefore, the area of consideration in this volume is highly significant. The author deserves all encomiums for his labour in addressing such a significant area affecting human society. The book would delight not only scholars but also those who care to know the nature and determinants of value formation. I bless Afzalur Rahman once again and I am sure he has a glorious future ahead.

Dulumoni Goswami,
Ph.D.
Associate Professor
Department of Education
Gauhati University

Preface

Value literally means something that has a price, something precious and worthwhile. This may be material or concrete aspects as well as non-material or abstract concepts like state of mind, interests, truthfulness, peace, happiness etc. Different philosophies, theories and views associated with values- Eastern as well as Western, though differ widely, have come to a point of consensus that values are the normative ethics which guide us to decide what is right, good, desirable, ought to be and vice-versa and serve as the grounds for our decision-making process and the final course of action. A vibrant set of values provide the basis for principles of life that give direction and firmness to life and bring joy, satisfaction, peace and quality to life in the same way as the rail keep a train on the track and help it move smoothly and quickly with direction.

But, unfortunately in modern times the valuing of men has shifted from spiritualism to materialism, from humanism to barbarism. The material pursuit has become the be-all and end-all of life. With the advancement of science and technology in the twenty-first century, the civilisation has conquered the moon but simultaneously the barbaric and valueless tendencies are dominating our lives. India is a country with diversified culture which is rich in its traditional beliefs and value systems. The ancient Indian system of education entirely concentrated on moral and spiritual development of minds. The whole of Vedic education and even the Post-Vedic lectures like the Ramayana, the Mahabharata, the Geeta etc. are the treasure house of values. The holy Quran also stresses the importance of human values. The importance of value education has also been duly recognised by different committees and commissions on education appointed in India so far.

But in spite of the steady efforts, value education is being neglected to a great extent. Our present educational system with all its complexities and niceties, have proved to be deficient so far, as it neglects or does not give deserving importance to values in human life. The prime objective of education today is no longer the formation of character and promotion of values, but the emphasis is on promotion of technical knowhow, skills, and technologies for material progress.

Thus, there is considerable debate among all sections of the society about the influence of professionalisation of education, among others, in transforming the native Indian values rooted on humanitarianism and pluralism into concrete and materialistic values. Most often it is argued that professional education increases the aspiration level of students in concrete aspects which in turn affects the value system of the professionals, since high level of aspiration sometimes forces individuals to change their value pattern in specific situations. The personality or self concept becomes concrete by the time students enter professional courses after plus two stage. Thus, there might have some sort of relationship among values, aspirations and professional education that needs to be investigated scientifically to reduce the knowledge gap in this regard. The present book intends to do the same and as such entitled as *'Values, Aspiration and Professional Education: A Predictive Analysis among Undergraduate Students.'*

The book is based on the dissertation leading to the degree of Doctor of Philosophy in Education conferred to Dr. Afzalur Rahman by the Gauhati University in the year 2014. The original title of the dissertation is 'A Study on the Value Dimensions of Undergraduate Students of Professional Courses in Relation to their Level of Aspiration'. The research work is carried out under the guidance of Dr. Dulumoni Goswami, Associate Professor of Education, Gauhati University. The research is quantitative in nature that tried to investigate the value dimensions and level of aspiration of undergraduate students of professional courses involving a relationship between the two variables and prediction of the former by the later. The study also analyses the gender differences and difference between the students of technical professional and non-technical professional courses in terms of the selected variables in order to have a micro level understanding of the process of value formation. The book is divided in to five chapters. First chapter deals with the theoretical orientation of values and level of aspiration, involving justification and objectives of the research work. The second chapter depicts critical review of related literature incorporating a systematic trend analysis. The research methods find place in third chapter. The fourth chapter deals with analysis of data and discussion of results. Finally the fifth chapter includes major findings, suggestions and conclusion. Considering the quantum of research work and input to the area of values, level of aspiration and professional education the present book is expected to motivate its readers, especially the researchers and administrators to develop its propagation and impel motivation for further research.

I take this opportunity to extend my sincere gratitude to my parents, my brothers, my wife, in-laws and all those from whom I have received support and encouragement to accomplish the work. My special thanks go to Dr. Dulumoni Goswami, Associate Professor, Department of Education, Gauhati University without the guidance, support and encouragement of whom, the work would not have been possible. My thanks go to all the teachers of Education Department of Gauhati University, Principal of my working college and all the colleagues of my department and college for their valued suggestions.

I extend my special thanks to Shri. Amit Garg, Director Kalpaz Publications, New Delhi and all the employees for taking cognizance for publishing my research work in readable book and bringing out this on time. I do look forward to any suggestions from my readers for further improvement of the book.

Afzalur Rahman, Ph.D.

List of Tables

List of Figures

Chapter – 1

Introduction

1.1 Introduction

God's best creature none but men and women alone can realise as well as practise spirituality and supreme values in their behaviour to the highest perfection. The pride possession of character is the most worthwhile, and inseparable to human beings like brightness inseparable to diamond. The human race, indeed, is the custodian of the most precious gift of God i.e. Purity in speech, thought and action, without which no civilisation could ever be complete. In fact, the concept of moral, spiritual and human values has been prevailing on earth since long as the human being exists. It has been carried out by human society to regulate their behaviour in relation to other. The human beings are continually valuing things and activities throughout their whole life. But, in modern times, the valuing of men has shifted from spiritualism to materialism, from humanism to barbarism. The material pursuit has become the be-all and end-all of life. The present era has witnessed serious erosion of moral virtues and human values.

Someone very truly said that if a tree reaches the sky (Heaven) its root might reach the Hell. With the advancement of science and technology, today the civilisation have conquered the moon but simultaneously the barbaric qualities like selfishness, clashes, corruption, nepotism, hypocrisy etc. are dominating our lives. The twenty-first century is jeopardised by valueless tendencies like corruption, violence, immorality, terrorism, crime, murder, rape, agitation, self-centred egoism, youth unrest, eve-teasing, degenerating civil services, exploitation in all walks of life, growing pollution of all types etc. Human virtues like love, sympathy, honesty, purity of mind, selflessness, wisdom, mercy, humility, faithfulness, obedience, sincerity etc. remain only the words of dictionary. Science and technology opened up new vistas as a result of which rapid and visible changes have been taken place extensively in almost all walks of human activity and endeavour. But, the most precious wealth of humanity that we lost today is a big measure of our character, ethics and values. It is said that if an individual loses his wealth, he loses nothing; if he loses his health, he loses something; but if he loses his character, he loses everything. What is true of individuals is also true of nations (Kapur, J. N., 2000).

Considering the present value crisis ridden atmosphere, *Bhagban Baba* in his Benedictory address at the Eighth Convocation, November 22, 1989 stated that,

> *"Wealth is worshipped as God. Pride has become a creed. Selfishness is entrenched in the intellect. The ego is flaunted and Desire has become an adornment. Righteousness has become a mere figures head in the world. Compassion has dried up. Gratitude has wanted. Hypocrisy has become the hallmark of life. Love and affection have become lustful affections. The scriptures are disregarded....In the Kali age these have become the qualifications of educated persons".*
>
> (Chittibabu, S.V., 2000)

The world wide resurgence of interest in value education is indicative of the fact that value crisis is not only a phenomenon of a particular country but the whole world is witnessing tremendous value crisis. India is a country of diversified culture which is rich in its traditional beliefs and value systems. It is the land which was known as the custodian of 'soul' in the ancient lore, is becoming a nation without soul now. Materialism has engulfed us to the extent that everyone by and large has become a worshipper of mammon (Dixit, P., 1998). *'Sattyam, Shivam, Sundaram'* meaning Truth, Beauty and Goodness were the highest values cherished in ancient India that had guided the human life towards attainment of Moksha. The Ancient Indian system of education entirely concentrated on moral and spiritual development of minds. The whole of Vedic education and even the Post-Vedic lectures like the Ramayana, the Mahabharata, the Geeta etc. are the treasure house of values. The holy Quran also stresses the importance of human values. The Islamic approach for the establishment of peace and welfare of humanity emphasises on the establishment of social peace, moderation and snubbing all destructive activities and permitting only the positive actions (Pakeeza and Chishti, 2012). But unfortunately, the continuity of our great cultural tradition was precluded by the long-stretched rule over the country by foreigners. Technological advances and the growing materialism have deprived people from the essence of India's ancient value system. After independence considerable advancement have taken place in almost all endeavours like agriculture, industry, science and technology, education etc., but Indians are losing their character, pride and identity of values. The present Indian society is characterised by speedy erosion of moral, social, spiritual and religious values, which are creating serious threats to the standards of personal and social life as well as the progress of the nation at large. Goswami, Dulumoni (2011), in his book *"Higher Education in India—Growth, Issues and Expansion*" has mentioned some matters arousing out of the effects of value crisis in the present day life. A few of them are as follows:

- The democratic ideology that has been accepted by our country is yet to be actualised in the form of social and economic democracy, so as to realise the democratic values guaranteed by the constitution of India.
- A new impersonal social order that is developing fast has been unduly ignoring the values and concepts without attempting to replace them with suitable ones.
- The individual is becoming a prey to contradictory values and ideologies and is being converted as a consequence in to an extreme radical, a reactionary, a sceptic or a cynic.
- Our curriculum does not reflect values and value system. Hence, our schools and colleges have become examination centres and not value centres.

In such a fissiparous situation, therefore, if hoped to create an enlightened and spiritual society, we the citizens should concentrate not only on our personal welfare but also for the good of others. We should not be indifferent towards altruism and interests of other people. The objective of creating an enlightened human society can be achieved only when the human possessions like health, harmony, happiness, wisdom and above all character reflecting ethical and human values will manifest in every one's thought, speech and action.

1.2. Values: The Concept, Classification and Determinants

Value literally means something that has a price, something precious and worthwhile. This may be material or concrete aspects as well as non-material or abstract concepts like state of mind, interests, truthfulness, peace, happiness etc. A newborn baby values his mother or the feeding bottle. As the infant grows into a boy or girl playthings acquire all the values. Similarly, in adulthood friends are replaced by a married partner in life. But, besides the possession of things or persons like mother, feeding bottle, doll, marbles, bats, balls, friends, house, furniture, jewellery, children and grand children; values extend to what we want to become or desire to be (Prahallada, N. N., 2000). We value what we desire to have or become and hence become the ideals, standards and set of guiding principles of all our activities and endeavour. In this connection the statement made by John Dewey is worth mentioning which states that *"The value means primarily to prize, to esteem, to appraise and to estimate. It means the act of achieving something, holding it dear and also the act of passing judgement upon the nature and amounts of values as compared with something else."* (Aggarwal, J.C., 2010)

The word 'value' is derived from the Latin word 'Valerie' which means to be strong and vigorous. Thus, 'to be of value' implies to have certain virtues. 'Axiology', the branch of philosophy is concerned with the study of values. However, history shows that the philosophers of the great tradition from Plato to Hegel have been greatly concerned with values, though they may not use the term value, but have spoke of desires and aims. There are altogether four views regarding the nature of values namely the *Interest theory, Existence theory, Experimental theory and Part-Whole theory* (Jangaiah, C., 1998).

The *Interest theory* is also known as subjective theory. According to this theory, if a person desires something it has a value for him/her.

Value resides in the inner world of mind and depends upon the interest of persons. The activity or event which is interesting or satisfactory for an individual is valuable or worthwhile for him/her but may not for others. It is idealistic in nature.

Secondly, the *Existence theory* is objective in nature. It holds that value is independent of the subject or his/her interest and mind, rather it wholly belong to the object. This theory believes that value is entirely manifested in the outer world which needs to be discovered for making judgement. This theory is realistic in nature.

Thirdly, the *Experimental theory* advocates that the thing or event which yields a greater sense of happiness at present and promises still more of it in future only holds value. Experimental value can also be interpreted as the instrumental value, which helps in the achievement of certain fruitful end but not permanent or absolute. This value is the outcome of pragmatic philosophy.

Lastly, the *Part-Whole theory* holds that in order to realise and enjoy value, one must effectively relate parts to the whole.

According to Indian philosophy which is not completely free from the hold of religion, the value is associated with the activities or endeavours that are directed towards spiritual liberation (Moksha). The four Purusharthas i.e. Supreme ends of life which hold highest value in Indian philosophy are Economic Well Being (Artha), Physical Wellbeing (Kama), Righteous Action (Dharma) and Spiritual Freedom (Moksha). Of the four, Artha and Kama are treated as relatively lower value than Dharma and Moksha. Economic Well being (Artha) and Physical Well being (Kama) are to be achieved through Righteous Action (Dharma), which in turn help in the realisation of the ultimate end of life i.e. Moksha. Thus, Dharma is considered as regulatory principle of attaining Artha and Kama in proximate sense and Moksha in ultimate sense. On the contrary, western view holds that value judgement is not necessarily dependent on religion, rather it is completely a rational activity and guided by reason. When an individual decides an action to be right or wrong; some course of action as ought to be followed or ought not to be, implies that these judgements are backed by reason behind these (Goyal, B. R., 1998).

Thus, it is seen that values have been conceptualised in a large number of perspectives and in a variety of ways. And as such, defining values inclusively have always been a big problem before philosophers, psychologists, sociologists and all concerned intellectuals. Morris (1957) had accepted value as indefinable. However, the definition given by *Kluckhohn* (1960) stating value as *"A conception, explicit or implicit, distinctive of an individual or characteristics of a group of those desirables which influence the selection, from available means and ends of action"* seems to be most inclusive of all, as it recognises the relationship between subjective and objective views of values, and values as both personal and societal.

Thus, almost all types of concepts viewed values in terms of normative ethics which guide us to decide what is right, desirable, ought to be and vice-versa. It refers to an internal code or mechanism that enables us to distinguish between good and bad, right and wrong, desirable and undesirable, justice and injustice and serves as a ground for our decision-making process and the final course of action. It is the norm that helps people to formulate judgments and to select the most sound and appropriate course of action that is acceptable by the society and culture to which they belong. Values create a specific mode of conduct and our end-state of existence and motivate, define and colour all our activities Cognitive, Affective and Psycho-motor. In this way, a vibrant set of values provide the basis for principles of life that give direction and firmness to life and bring joy, satisfaction, peace and quality to life in the same way as the rail keep a train on the track and help it move smoothly and quickly with direction without accident. Value is an abstract concept and regarded desirable, important and held in high esteem by a particular society in which a person lives (Venkataiah, N., 1998).

Values are classified differently by different thinkers according to their own way on the basis of some specific criteria. Most of the schools of philosophy are agreed to classify values into two types as higher and lower values. For example, knowledge is considered as higher value in comparison to physical pleasure. *Turner,* classified values as abstract and concrete. According to *Spindler* values are of two types as traditional and emergent. Traditional value stands for concepts like puritan morality, work success ethics, individualism and achievement orientation. On the other hand, emergent value is used to mean qualities like sociability, moral attitude, consideration for others, and conformity to groups etc. Sprenger, Edward (1928), in his book *"Type of Men"* mentioned six values as theoretical, economic, aesthetic, social, political and religious. According to Brubacher (1962), values are of two fold, Terminal and Instrumental. Terminal values are those basic values of life that include survival, caring, comfort, dignity, freedom, knowledge, self-respect etc. These are rooted in human nature and are judged good not for others else, but in and out of themselves. These values are inherent, self-contained and end in themselves. They represent the ultimate life-goals that people have. On the other hand, instrumental values are not self-contained and inherent, but are associated with some other values. Instrumental or intermediate values serve as a means of attaining the fundamental or basic values. These instrumental values include moral, social and spiritual values. These are judged good not for themselves, rather because they are good for something else and help to promote the ultimate life-goals of people. Indian philosophy classified values into four types which are called 'Purusharthas' viz., Dharma, Artha, Kama and Moksha. Dharma and Moksha are viewed as supreme values where Artha and Kama are viewed as lower values. Similarly, Artha and Kama are held as temporary values, whereas Dharma and Moksha are held as permanent and absolute values because Artha and Kama through Dharma (Righteous action) help in attainment of Moksha i.e. spiritual freedom.

Further, classifications of values have been made from time to time, but no classification seems to be conclusive. However, all efforts are focused to explain cherished experiences related to human ideas and aspirations. In total, a well defined value system is a mirror-image of an individual's character, perception of well-being and determines his short and long-range purposes, goals and priorities. Indeed, irrespective of divergence in classification, there is a consensus that Sattyam, Shivam and Sundaram (truth, goodness and beauty) are the highest combination of values. These are considered desirable and help in achieving a better world as well as the ultimate end of life.

Underlying much of the research studies it is implicit that value dimensions are essentially related, influenced and shaped by factors like sex; age; marital status; psychological and personality traits like interest, aptitude, motivation, intelligence, achievement motivation, self-concept etc; socio-economic status; parental education and expectation; rearing up practice; home environment; area of residence; culture; religion; education and school climate etc. (refer Chapter-II). Students persuing different types of education may possess different value pattern as education system is one of the most potent factors in determining values of individual. Similarly, students with different levels of aspiration may also differ in their value patterns. Level of aspiration is closely associated with value dimensions in the sense that it may determine or may be determined by value dimensions. The following paragraph discusses the second variable of the present study i.e. level of aspiration.

1.3. Level of Aspiration: The Concept, Determinants and Development

The dictionary meaning of the word aspiration is 'to desire eagerly to a certain standard, to aim at or strive for certain higher goals and to tower up'. To 'aspire' means 'to desire', this is a pre-requisite of any achievement. Level of aspiration is an individual's future expectation or ambition. Dembo, who was a student of Lewin, first introduced the concept of level of aspiration in 1931 in the course of an experimental investigation of anger. The word 'aspiration' is a translation from German word 'Ansprush' and 'Niveau'.

The first experiment directed towards the analysis of level of aspiration was performed by Hoppe in 1930. Hoppe defined level of aspiration as a person's expectations, goals or claims on his own future achievement in a given task. He opined that level of aspiration is qualitative in nature because on the basis of his experiment, he found that a given performance is accompanied by a feeling of failure if it falls below the level of aspiration and a given performance is accompanied by a feeling of success if it goes above the level of aspiration. Hoppe further investigated various factors which effect goal setting behaviour. He concluded that individual variations are found in level of aspiration. In his view, a realistic person always set a goal on the basis of his past experience keeping in view of his capabilities for doing a particular task. Thus, Hoppe conceived level of aspirations a technique for studying dynamic factors which operate in the prediction of feeling of success and failure.

Frank (1935) altered Hoppe's concept of level of aspiration in the light of his quantitative technique, where the goodness of performance was measured in terms of the times taken to complete the set task. He redefined Hoppe's concept of level of aspiration as level of future performance in a familiar task which an individual, knowing his level of past performance in that task, explicitly undertakes to reach. Frank emphasised the role of ego-involvement in determining one's level of aspiration and concluded that the degree of ego-involvement is correlated with divergence of level of aspiration.

According to Dembo (1931), an individual's aspiration level represents him/her not only as he/she is at that particular moment but also as he/she would like to be. It is a measure of his internal dispositions. According to Boyd (1952), level of aspiration means an individual's ambition in a dynamic situation i.e. it is an individual's goal or expectation with regard to the goodness of his own future performance for a given task. Backer and Seigal (1957) referred level of aspiration, 'as individual strives for a particular goal or level of achievement.'

In the words of Hurlock (1967), aspiration means, "a longing for what is above one's achieved level with advancement on its end. In other words aspiration means the goal an individual sets for himself in a task, which has intense personal significance for him and in which he is ego-involved."

Scanning the foregoing definitions, it appears that level of aspiration is a form of self motivation involving competition with one's past experience. When an individual is actively involved in a task, he sets new goal to achieve. If he succeeds in attaining the set goal, it motivates him to set higher goal in the subsequent attempts besides giving him satisfaction. On the other hand, if he fails to attain his set goal, he experiences a sense of failure which is normally followed by a lowering of the goal for future attempts. This is a common characteristic of behaviour in all goal setting situations.

Level of aspiration is usually influenced by two types of factors- environmental and personal. Environmental factors include determinants like parental ambitions, social expectations, peer pressure, social value, education, competition, group cohesiveness etc. In early childhood, before the child is old enough to know what his abilities, interests and values are, his aspirations are largely shaped by environment. On the other hand, personal factors play dominant role in determining his level of aspiration as the child grows older and become more aware of his abilities and interests. These personal factors include determinants such as wishes, personality traits, past experiences, values, interests, sex, socio-economic background, racial background etc. Gutman, L. M. and Akerman, R. (2008) stated that aspirations begin to be shaped early in a child's life and tend to decline as children become mature. They further concluded that practical and attitudinal factors play important role in preventing high aspiration among individuals. Financial constraints, earlier failure in academic achievement, becoming parents at younger stage etc. are some of the practical problems which act as barrier in the formation of aspiration. They further showed that the individuals, who are confident in their ability to achieve and attribute their success to hard work and not on luck, tend to form higher aspirations.

Generally, a great deal of individual differences is found in goal setting behaviour. Even persons with equal amount of ability may also differ significantly in their level of aspiration. One may set his goal very high, while some other very low and some may have aspiration level near to their performance level or capacity. Setting ones goal and level of aspiration in accordance with socio-economic as well as psycho-physical condition is of vital importance for balanced development of personality. A congenial and conducive environment both at home and school and exemplary behaviour of family members and teachers goes a long way in setting aspiration level suited to one's capacity as well as helps in fostering right value in children at large.

1.4. Formation of Values as a Function of Education

The principal objective of education is to bring all round development of the personality. It needs not necessarily to focus on merely providing certain degrees or diplomas. Education has to integrate all the dimensions of personality- mental, social, moral, spiritual, physical and so on along with developing human values which are desirable for the individual as well as for the society. In fact, education itself is a social process as it goes in the social set up and meant for preparing the individual for effective social living with other fellow members. Its function is to transmit, preserve and promote the desirable aspects of culture, ideals and norms of society from one generation to another. It is to instil in the minds of the students a sense of morality and concern for others. It has to develop among the students the power to distinguish between right and wrong, desirable and undesirable, justice and injustice etc. Thus, good education, its aim, curriculum, methods of education, role of teachers etc. all are always inseparably tied up with inculcation of universal and eternal values. Real education should combine science and ethics, and create a passionate hunger for truth.

In ancient days the word 'value' was not being affixed before 'education'. The term 'education' was quite sufficient to specify its function of value orientation. But today, everybody talk about value education, and the subject of value education is becoming increasingly prominent in educational discussion at all levels. Such extended emphasis on value orientation through education depicts how value is diminishing in the present society. All over the glove, the moral, spiritual and human values are getting relegated to the background. The minds are captivated to western culture. There is an unhealthy race among people behind the material wealth. The possibilities of earning more and more have dominating the younger minds. The twenty-first century is jeopardised with valueless and unethical activities in its entire dimensions— personal, social, political, economic etc. And the education is also unable to do what it is expected to do. It has become one sided. Rapid strives have been made in acquisition of knowledge about the outer world, in the growth of physical sciences, and in discovering the wonders of the materialistic means (Bhandari, M. S., 2000). Goswami, Dulumoni (2011) stated that values, attitude, interests, appreciations have come to be sidelined during recent times and education has become a process of acquisition of information in conventional cognitive areas with the sole purpose of passing the examinations. People have forgotten that knowledge which does not accompany wisdom will lead the human race only to barbarism and make them slaves of material civilisation. In this connection Russel, B. (1967) in his book *"Impact of Science in Society"*, says, *"Unless people increase in wisdom as much as in knowledge, increase of knowledge will be increase of sorrow*".

Indian education system since its inception has been emphasising the inculcation of right values in the growing minds. The whole of ancient system of education- the Vedic education, Buddhist system of education, education during Muslim era etc. are deeply rooted on value orientation. Holy Scriptures of all religions prevalent in the country like Hinduism, Islam, Christianity, Sikhism, Jainism, Buddhism etc. is treasure house of sound moral teachings. The modern system of education, before and after independence, has also been highlighting the urgent need for incorporating appropriate programmes in education for bringing integrated development of body, mind and spirit of the students. Prior to independence, the Central Advisory Board of Education (1943-46) suggested that provision of spiritual and moral instruction for building up the character of the young should be the responsibility of the home and community. As the country attained freedom from the British yoke, a new thought has aroused to reconstruct the education in consonance with the native value traditions so as to cope with the changing socio-economic and political system. Various committees and commissions being appointed thereafter, on education at all levels have duly recognised the importance of value orientation. Radhakrishna Commission (1948), Secondary Education Commission (1953), the Sri Prakasa Committee (1959), Kothari Commission (1964-66), National Policy on Education (1986), Ramamurti Committee (1990), Programme of Action (NPE) (1992) all have taken cognizance of the need for value orientation through education and recommended direct or indirect instruction of social, moral, and religious values in educational institutions. Some of the statements made in this direction are as follows:

Radhakrishnan Commission (1948): *"If we exclude spiritual training in our institutions we would be untrue to our whole historical development".*

Sri Prakasa Committee on Religious and Moral Instruction (1959): *"Every effort must, therefore, be made to teach students true moral values from the earliest stages of their educational life".*

Kothari Commission (1964-66): *"A serious defect in the school system is the absence of provision for education in social, moral and spiritual values. In the life of majority of Indians, religion is a great motivating force and is intimately bound up with the formation of character and inculcation of ethical values. A national system of education that is related to life, needs and aspirations of people cannot afford to ignore this purposeful force".*

National Policy on Education (1986): *"The growing concern over the erosion of essential values and an increasing cynicism in society has brought to focus the need for readjustments in the curriculum in order to make education a forceful tool for the cultivation of social and moral values."*

Ramamurti Committee (1990): *"Education must further provide a climate for the nurture of values, both as a personalised set of values, forming one's character and including necessarily social, cultural and national values, so as to have a context and meaning for actions and decisions, and in order to enable the persons to act with conviction and commitment".*

Programme of Action (NPE) (1992): *"The framework emphasised value education as an integral part of school curriculum. It highlighted the values drawn from national goals, universal perception, ethical considerations and character building. It stressed the role of education in combating obscurantism, religious fanaticism, exploitation and injustice as well as the inculcation of values".*

But, in spite of the steady efforts, value education is being neglected to a great extent. It is much pity that nothing is done sincerely and dedicatedly in this direction in India till date. Education in general and higher education in particular, which is considered as the most potent factor in value orientation, has failed today in its sole purpose. It proved quite ineffective in recent times to inculcate among the young generation the values such as love, co-operation, trust, acceptance, joy, dignity, compromise, respect for others, sympathy, tolerance, forgiveness which are the backbone of society. The majority of educational institutions have failed in evolving an integrated approach in the curricular and co-curricular programmes for the all round development of human personality. The system with all its complexities and intricacies, have proved to be deficient so far, as it neglects or does not give deserving importance to values in human life (Venkataiah, N., 1998). It is becoming day by day more or less materialistic and value traditions are being slowly given up. The prime objective of education today is no longer the formation of character and promotion of values, but the emphasis is on promotion of technical knowhow, skills, and technologies for material progress.

As the labour market is becoming more specified, it requires more skilled person in different profession. Consequently, professional education is becoming more popular in this age of LPG. The emergence of private sector in education, more particularly at tertiary level, has made the system mostly commercial. Now, education is considered as instruments for preparing the students as money earning tools. Provision of value education seldom exists in institutions of professional courses run by private undertakings. Profit-motive always remain their first priority. No doubt, in a country like India where unemployment rate is almost 10 per cent, career oriented professional education is of utmost significance. But, at the same time such career oriented professional education must take cognizance to instruct the students in desirable human values. It is very unfortunate that Modern Indians are being educated mainly with the bread and butter aim of education, as a result, most of our graduates run after money, power, comforts without caring for any values (Prahallada, N. N., 2000). Thus, there is an urgent need to revive and reform the values of human life and to rejuvenate the foundation of civilisation. It is vitally necessary for the universities to consider their special role in education in human values. Institutions of higher education might have to function properly in transforming cultural heritage, accumulated knowledge, values and skills from one generation to the other. In the present value crisis-ridden society education must create the climate for the nurture of values.

1.5. Objectives of the Study

(i) To study the value preferences of undergraduate students of both technical and non-technical professional courses of Gauhati University.

(ii) To examine whether there is significant difference between undergraduate students of technical and non-technical professional courses in their value dimensions.

(iii) To study the level of aspiration of undergraduate students of both technical and non-technical professional courses of Gauhati University.

(iv) To determine the relationship between value dimensions and level of aspiration of undergraduate students of technical and non-technical professional courses.

(v) To determine the relationship between value dimensions and level of aspiration of male and female undergraduate students of professional courses.

(vi) To examine whether there is significant difference in the relationship of value dimensions and level of aspiration between undergraduate students of technical and non-technical professional courses.

(vii) To examine whether there is significant difference in the relationship of value dimensions and level of aspiration between male and female undergraduate students of professional courses.

(viii) To study the level of aspiration as predictor of value dimensions of undergraduate students of both technical and non-technical professional courses.

1.6. Hypotheses of the Study

The following hypotheses have been formulated in order to meet the objectives.

Ho_1: There is no significant difference between undergraduate students of technical and non-technical professional courses in their value dimensions.

Ho_2: There is no significant difference between undergraduate students of technical and non-technical professional courses in their level of aspiration score.

Ho_3: There is no significant relationship between value dimensions and level of aspiration of undergraduate students of technical and non-technical professional courses.

Ho_4: There is no significant relationship between value dimensions and level of aspiration of male and female undergraduate students of professional courses.

Ho_5: There is no significant difference in the relationship of value dimensions and level of aspiration between undergraduate students of technical and non-technical professional courses.

Ho_6: There is no significant difference in the relationship of value dimensions and level of aspiration between male and female undergraduate students of professional courses.

H_7: Level of aspiration is the predictor of value dimensions of undergraduate students of both technical and non-technical professional courses.

1.7. Significance of the Study

Today there is almost a public debate on the erosion of values. Newspapers, magazines and other news media are flooded with the news of immoral and criminal activities which are creating serious threats for the smooth survival of mankind. So, it becomes important for all the members of the society to understand the nature of values and factors responsible for its formation and development.

There is a general feeling that our present system of education is not quite effective in inculcating the right values among the young generation. It is becoming more materialistic day by day and value traditions are being slowly given up. The prime objective of education today is no longer the formation of character and promotion of values, rather the emphasis is on promotion of technical knowhow, skills, and technologies for material progress. The students of today are primarily inclined towards the fulfilment of material greed. So far the students of undergraduate level of education are concerned; there is considerable paucity of research attempts on value dimensions in India in general and in Assam in particular. It is evident from the overview of the review of related studies, that only one study is made in Assam by Islam, Sirajul (2002) to examine the value pattern of college students. Considering the inadequacy, the importance of the present study aiming at identification of value dimensions of undergraduate students of professional courses as well as their determining factors is justified.

Professional education has been recognised as inevitable for a country's socio-economic development. Though, the main motto of professional education is to prepare students for job, simultaneously it must teach the students the desirable human values. Research studies on professional education undertaken in some foreign countries and also in India mostly covered the areas like management, administration, job satisfaction, vocational preference etc. The value pattern of students of professional courses received little or no attention by scholars. Among the related literature reviewed, only one study investigating the attitudes, self-concept and values of Professional and Non-professional college students is found which was conducted by Manav, Ram Niwas (1981) under Meerut University. No study involving a comparison on value dimensions of students of technical and non-technical professional courses has been conducted so far. Therefore, this neglected area of professional education needs to be addressed with great care.

In today's world of competition, there is not a single individual who is devoid of ambition in some or other form. Everyone seems to set their aspiration to a higher level. At the same time, the whole world is witnessing tremendous value crisis. Thus, natural questions arise whether our value dimensions are shaped and influenced by our level of aspiration? Is there any relationship between level of aspiration and value dimensions of individuals? Level of aspiration is closely associated with value dimensions in the sense that it may determine or may be determined by value dimensions. It is observed in the overview of related literature scanned, that value dimensions are not adequately investigated in relation to level of aspiration. One study is made by Ranu, Sarbjit Kaur (1995) in Patiala on value pattern of postgraduate students in relation to level of aspiration. No study is found revealing the value dimensions in relation to their level of aspiration so far undergraduate students of professional courses is concerned. As such the necessity of conducting the present study is felt important.

Considering the above issues, the importance of the present study is justified. This is an attempt to throw light on this neglected area of professional education. The study is first of its kind and as such is expected to fill the gap in this regard.

1.8. Operational Definition of Important Terms

In order to make the research precise and convenient and also to avoid any ambiguity, the operational definitions of important terms used, are given below.

(1) Value Dimensions

Value Dimensions refers to the six types of values as measured by R.K. Ojha and Mahesh Bhargava's revised form of 'Study of Values Test', an adaptation of Allport-Vernon-Lindzey Scale of values, used in the present study. These value dimensions are-

(i) **Theoretical:** The dominant interest of the theoretical man is the *Discovery of Truth* and *Empirical, Rational and Critical* treatment of issue.

(ii) **Economic:** The economic man is characteristically interested in what is *Useful, Economic* or *Profitable* for him. These men are thoroughly '*Practical*'.

(iii) **Aesthetic:** The aesthetic man sees his highest value in *Form and Harmony*.

(iv) **Social:** The highest value for this type of man is *Love of People*.

(v) **Political:** The political man is interested primarily in *Power and Influence*.

(vi) **Religious:** The highest value of religious man is *Unity*. They are *mystical* and seek to comprehend the cosmos as a whole.

(2) Level of Aspiration

Level of aspiration is an individual's future expectation or ambition in a given task. In the present study, it refers to the aspiration level of an individual as revealed by his total GDS (Goal Discrepancy Score) on the 'Level of Aspiration Measure' developed by Mahesh Bhargava and Late Professor M. A. Shah.

(3) Undergraduate Students

Undergraduate Students refers to the students studying for their first degree in all the degree colleges affiliated to Gauhati University offering education in professional courses.

(4) Professional Education

Professional Education refers to those subjects or streams of study that prepares students to become extremely competent for a job through giving specialised training to engage in an activity, the purpose of which is to supply objective counsel and service to others for gaining direct and definite compensation or a means of livelihood.

In the present study 'Professional Education' covers the subjects or streams of study like Engineering, Education, Medicine, Technology, Law, Management, Architecture, Town Planning, Pharmacy, Applied Arts & Crafts, Hotel Management and Catering Technology etc.

(5) Technical Professional Course

Technical Course refers to those subjects or streams of study that makes academic and vocational preparation of students for jobs that are based on practical activities involving applied science and modern technology where emphasis is given to the understanding and practical application of basic principles of science and mathematics, rather than the attainment of proficiency in manual skills that is properly the concern of vocational education.

In the present study the researcher has used the term 'Technical Professional Course' to mean those professional subjects or stream of study which are under the purview of AICTE. These are Engineering, Technology, Management, Architecture, Town Planning, Pharmacy, Applied Arts & Crafts, Hotel Management and Catering Technology.

(6) Non-Technical Professional Course

Non-Technical Course refers to the subjects or stream of study that prepares students to become competent for a job through giving specialised training to earn his livelihood that do not necessarily involve applied science and modern technology and an understanding and practical application of basic principles of science and mathematics.

In the present study the term 'Non-Technical Professional Course' refers to all other professional subjects or stream of study like Medicine, Education, Law, Music etc., except those which are under the purview of AICTE.

Chapter – 2

Review of Related Literature

A thorough review of related literature helps the researcher to proceed in a logical sequence and produce fruitful results as it makes the researcher perceive what is already done in the field concerned and what needs to be done. It helps in recognising the research gap through trend analysis and finally assists in identifying exactly the problem that needs immediate attention. In this way, the review of earlier studies helps to develop a perspective to ascertain the general trend in the area, to locate the unexplored problems, and thereby avoids unnecessary duplication of the study. Furthermore, critical analysis of related literature provides assistance in formulating the research problem, specifying objectives, making useful hypotheses, developing theoretical background, use of proper methodology and drawing meaningful conclusions and generalisations. Review of related literature, therefore, is the pre-requisite for any scientific investigation as it provides direction and guidance to research in the same way as history corrects and guides us from many pitfalls.

Recognising the importance, effort has been made to present the review of related studies available in the form of theses, dissertations, journals, books, etc. The literatures related to the present study are presented in chronological order under the following heads.

- Studies done in India
- Studies done Abroad.

2.1. Studies Done in India

Manav, Ram Niwas (1981) made an attempt to study the attitudes, Self-concept and values of Professional and Non-professional college students. The study revealed significant difference between professional and non-professional students with regard to personal, religious, materialistic and humanistic values. The study further revealed that medical and engineering college students differ significantly in personal and social values; engineering and teacher training students differ significantly on personal, religious and humanistic values; whereas medical and teacher training students differ significantly with regard to personal, religious, educational and humanistic value dimensions.

Sati, B. D. (1991) conducted a comparative study of needs, values, aspirations and adjustments of scheduled caste and other students of secondary schools of Kumaun. The findings showed that scheduled caste boys and scheduled caste girls did not differ on value preferences and on educational aspiration. But, non-scheduled caste boys and girls differed significantly in two value dimensions namely theoretical value and social value. In theoretical value non-scheduled caste boys were significantly better than their female counterparts, whereas in social value the non-scheduled caste girls were significantly better.

Bauni, Kuotsu (1992), has made an attempt to study the values of college students in Nagaland in relation to their self-concept. The study revealed that there was no significant difference in the mean scores of arts, science and commerce college students with respect to social, aesthetic, economic, knowledge hedonistic and health value scores, but boys and girls differed significantly with respect to their mean scores on social, aesthetic, knowledge power and family prestige values. There were significant differences between tribal and non-tribal students with respect to their mean scores on religious, social, aesthetic and domestic value.

Chuttaura, P. (1992) explored the adjustment, aspiration and value pattern of scheduled caste and scheduled tribe student-teachers of Rajasthan. The study found that the most preferred values of both scheduled caste and scheduled tribe teacher trainees were moral value followed by social value and that their least preferred values were economic followed by aesthetic value.

Jafri, Bilkis Sultana (1992) in her comparative study of Values and Aspirations of undergraduate women students between two colleges, found that the students of Arts Stream of Tika Ram College were significantly higher in values as compared to the students of Women's college, while the aspirations of students of Women's College was higher as compared to the students of Tika Ram College. The study also revealed the existence of significant difference in the aspiration and values between arts and science students, between high and low educated parental groups as well as between high and low parental income groups.

Padmanaban, T. A. (1992) in his study of values of high school pupils had revealed that there was a wide variety in different value scores where students scored higher in social value and lowest in political values. Boys and girls differed in their value pattern and caste and religion showed positive relationship with students value pattern.

Pradhan, G. C. (1992) in his study of values among secondary school students found that socio-economic status was significantly (positively) correlated with social, economic, knowledge, power, and family prestige values. Again moral judgement was positively correlated with religious, social, democratic, knowledge and health values while negatively correlated with economic, hedonistic, power and family prestige values. Moral judgement had no significant correlation with aesthetic value. The study further revealed significant sex differences in social, democratic, power and health values. Boys had higher democratic and health values than girls, while girls were higher on social and power values.

Shah, H. M. (1992) made an investigation into the values of higher secondary school students of Saurashtra. In this study Shah showed that sex, residential area, stream of the study had significant relationship with the values of students studying in class XI and XII. The study further revealed that stream or branch of study was significantly related to social value.

Shivamurti, Ansari and Venkataranganaika (1992) investigated the value orientation, Knowledge and adoption behaviour of sericulturists in Dharwad district of Karnataka. The findings revealed that social values play an important role in one's own life and acts as a driving force. The results showed that sericulturists with progressive values had high knowledge and adaptation behaviour. Thus, the researcher concluded that possession of progressive values help individuals to more forward towards new experiences leading to recognition.

Kaur, Amarjeet (1993) compared the value dimensions of 300 government and private senior secondary school students on A-V-L scale. The study revealed that government school boys preferred aesthetic and social values most and their least preferred value was religious. In case of girls of government school also the first two preferred values were same as that of boys but their least preferred value was economic which was religious for private school girls. Significant difference was observed between male and female students of government school with respect to three value dimensions namely economic, theoretical and religious. Boys were significantly higher in economic value than their counterparts whereas girls were higher than the boys in theoretical and religious value dimensions. With regard to students of private school, significant difference was noted in only in religious value dimension where females were significantly higher than the boys. No other sex difference was found in the other five value-dimensions so far students of private school were concerned.

Kaur, Amarpreet (1993) made a comparative study of value dimensions of post-graduate arts and science students. The study revealed that males in the science group had higher mean scores on theoretical, economic and political values than their counterparts in the arts group who were higher on aesthetic, social and economic values than the male science group. It was also found that girls from the science stream preferred theoretical and religious values more than the girls of arts stream, while on the remaining four dimensions arts group outscored the science group.

Khanna, Neeta (1993) studied the value patterns of students studying in teacher training and general streams in a denominational institute. The study was delimited to five value dimensions namely Truth, Righteous Conduct, Peace, Love and Non-Violence. The findings confirmed significant difference between two groups with respect to truth and love values where the students studying in teacher training stream outscored the other group. No significant difference was observed between the two groups on the remaining three value dimensions.

Singh, Iqbal (1993) conducted a study to identify the value dimension of secondary school teachers in relation to their sex, age and experience. The findings showed that the subject's preference order of value dimensions was political, followed by theoretical, economic, aesthetic, social and religious. The study further revealed significant sex difference with respect to five value dimensions. These were political, theoretical, economic, aesthetic, and religious values. The two most preferred values of less as well as more experienced teachers were found same. These were political followed by theoretical value.

Verma, V. P.; Das, Rajalakshmi and Swain, C. Bimal (1993) in their study of the main effect of sex and rural/urban inhabitation on the values of adolescent students found that male adolescents were higher on truth, non-violence and love value than female adolescents but no significant difference was observed between male and female subjects with respect to right conduct value and peace value. Again, on the variable of inhabitation all the F-ratios were found highly significant.

Narayanan, S.; Shantha K. D. K., Rao, K. S., and Kumar, K. G. (1994) conducted a study on value orientation among Indian and Singapore business students. The study focused on the cross-cultural differences in value orientation of these students. The analysis of the study revealed a trend towards materialistic value preferences by the Indian business students and more realistic value preferences by the Singapore business students. Indian students gave high importance to work and success, whereas the Singaporean students gave higher importance to love and life. The findings further revealed that self-concept, self-respect and health were assigned high ranks by both the groups of students.

Gurnani, L.; Bala, M., and Golwalkar, S. (1995) conducted a study to find out and compare the life values, personality and creativity among physically handicapped students and settled graduate persons. Comparison was made on 250 physically handicapped students drawn from Senior Secondary Schools of Rajasthan and 250 settled persons who had completed graduation and belonged to the age group of 25 to 40 years. The results related to values revealed that moral and aesthetic values were negatively related to all life values, except hedonistic value in respect of both physically handicapped students and settled persons. Moreover, the study did not find any relationship between flexibility and life value. The hedonistic value also did not show any relationship with creativity.

Ranu, Sarbjit Kaur (1995) in her study of value dimensions of post-graduate students in relation to their levels of aspiration and intelligence, found that the two most preferred value dimensions of post-graduate students were theoretical and political whereas two least preferred values were religious and aesthetic. The male students were significantly higher in theoretical value but, lower in aesthetic and social values than the female students. It is also found that arts students were significantly higher in aesthetic, social and political values than the science students. The study further revealed that level of aspiration and intelligence together were predictors of the scores among male and female students.

Taj, Haseen and Rekha, S. (1995) undertook an experimental design to find out whether the activities designed to inculcate the value of national integration had a strong influence in the development of national integration values. The study used the randomised control group post-test design. The analysis of results revealed that activities designed for had an influence in the development of national integration values.

Dhekwar, T. M. (1996) conducted a study on personality problems and value pattern of Higher Secondary students of non-technical course and vocational technical course. The study revealed that the hierarchy of values of H.S students of non-technical course and vocational technical course was similar in most of the cases. All groups of vocational technical course were higher in social and theoretical values. The study further revealed that religious and aesthetic values were held at low position by students of both non-technical and technical vocational course.

Verma, D. (1996), in his study on value pattern of 400 college students of Rohilkhand region with special reference to sense of responsibility, reflected that social values were higher among arts students and theoretical values among science and commerce students. The study further reported that the socio-economic status did not affect the values of college students and the streams of study (arts, science and commerce) did not differ significantly in their sense of responsibility.

Chauhan, V. L., and Kothari, P. (1997) in their paper studied the value patterns of 200 urban and rural women. A 2 X 2 X 2 factorial design with variables—type of area (rural vs urban), type of family (joint vs nuclear) and age at marriage (early vs late marriage) was adopted to assess the value pattern as a function of the mentioned variables. The results of ANNOVA revealed significant main effects of type of area on aesthetic, hedonistic, and health values; significant effect of the type of family on health values; and significant main effect of age at marriage on knowledge and health values.

Dagar, B. S., and Dhull, I. (1997) in their article stressed that value education in general and moral education in particular constitutes the *sine qua non* of education. The authors suggested the mode of moral education arguing that moral education is distinct from religious education while most often it is misinterpreted as religious education. They viewed that orientation of all working teachers on moral education through organising and conducting special seminars, orientation courses are a prerequisite for including moral education as a subject.

Gupta, S., and Mandal, J. M. (1997) studied the effects of education, location, sex and marital status on the terminal and instrumental values of 360 young men and women in the age group of 18 to 35 years. The samples were stratified according to sex, marital status, location (rural and urban) and education (fairly good educational background and poor educational background). Analysis of variance revealed that location, education, sex and marital status had a significant effect on the respondents' terminal values but not on their instrumental values.

Pradhan, G. C. (1997) conducted a study to explore the relationship between moral values with 10 personal values of 561 boy and girl school students of Puri district (Orissa). The results of Pearson's correlation revealed that moral judgement was positively correlated with religious, social, knowledge and health values, and was negatively correlated with personal and family-prestige values.

Pradhan, N. N., and Panda, A. K. (1997) in their study on the effects of tribal/ non-tribal status and sex on moral judgement among

42 tribal and 58 non-tribal children studying in class IX of three schools in the district of Koraput (Orissa) revealed existence of significant difference in moral judgement between both tribal and non-tribal as well as male and female school going children. Tribals compared to non-tribals, and boys compared to girls were at a higher stage of moral judgement.

Rao, G. B.; Reddy, K. S., and Samiuliah, S. (1997) investigated the work values of 120 employees from three different business organisations, in relation to their behaviour activity profiles i.e. Type 'A' and Type 'B' as measured by, Friedman and Rosenman, 1950. Results revealed that there were significant differences between the two types of individuals in the work values: creativity, management, supervisory relations, security, prestige, independence, variety, economic returns, altruism, and intellectual stimulation.

Ravindranathan, M. N. (1997) investigated the attitude of primary school teachers of Udupi town towards various educational, economic and religious aspects of life. The results of the analysis revealed that the majority of the primary school teachers of the Udupi town were modern in their attitude towards educational, economic and religious dimensions of life, which would have more modernising influence on all aspect of life of the young students.

Sharma, N. P. (1997) in this article argued that the task of teaching values to the young is the task of both parents and teachers. He holds that values are not fractional things to be doled out in fixed daily or weekly measures, as one among various subjects in the school syllabus. According to author, there are some specific values like good health, soundness of body and mind, honesty, truthfulness, equality, democracy, secularism and self-realisation that can be taught through formal education at all levels through incorporating games, sports, yoga and participative method of teaching values. Such a value as self-realisation can be self-taught through introspection, continuous practice, meditation and transcendence of the mundane realities.

In another study by Singh, A. K. and Gupta, Alpana Sen (1997) on the influence of personality and gender on value system of people found that neuroticism was positively related with theoretical, aesthetic and religious values whereas extraversion was positively related with social, political, and economic values. Females showed preferences for aesthetic, social, and religious values whereas males showed their preference for theoretical, political and economic values.

Singh, R. P. (1997) made an attempt to investigate the values of 560 urban and rural college going male and female adolescents of Aligarh district. The scale of value developed by Ray Chaudhary and R.K. Ojha was used in the study. The findings revealed that urban male and female had significantly higher mean scores on theoretical and religious value than the corresponding mean scores of rural male and female adolescents. On the other hand in social and aesthetic values the rural male and female adolescents had significantly higher mean scores than their counterparts, whereas in political and economic values mean difference of urban and rural adolescents were not significant. The study further reported that the male adolescents were significantly higher in the mean scores of theoretical and economic values than the female adolescent, whereas the female group was significantly higher on social and political values.

Singh, T., and Pathak, S. (1997) conducted an empirical study to explore the effect of residential background, age and gender on ecological attitude, value orientation and environmental perception in a sample of 180 people. Results indicated that rural people found nature as more positive, group-oriented, development and dominating; whereas factory people perceived nature as more unitary, organised and sensuous; with the perception of urban people falling between these extremes. The components of value orientation and ecological awareness were found to be significantly correlated.

Srivastava, S. K. (1997) studied the relationship between values and personality traits of 100 students of class IX drawn from two schools of Haridwar. The study showed that social and political values were positively correlated with the personality traits, whereas theoretical, economic, aesthetic and religious values did not show any significant relationship with the personality traits of students.

Pathak, R. D., and Tripathi, S. K. (1998) made an attempt to justify how modern information technology has influenced our values especially in the industrial sector. The authors stressed that the values which are getting abrasion are human values, community and social values, cultural values and institutional values etc. can be inculcated among the industrial personnel by organising various programmes such as symposia, seminars, and special lectures, and encouraging extra-curricular activities. They also suggested that value education should be a part of the curriculum of higher education.

Sahoo, K. C.; Biswal, A. and Khandai, H. (1998) investigated the perception of 225 students of different schools of DAV- Indore, about their existing secular values. The major findings reflected that secular value was prevalent among average number of university students. The study further revealed that scientific, humanitarian, moral, and spiritual values were high among the university students.

Bhagawati, Binita (1999) made a comparative analysis of value orientation in two school system of Assam (Vidya Bharati system and General school system). The findings revealed that the students of Vidya Bharati Schools secured higher scores on attitude scale of values than the General School system. Students of Vidya Bharati school system scored higher than their teachers but, there was no difference in the value scores between students and teachers of General Schools. The study further revealed that female students as well as female parents scored consistently higher than their male counterparts.

Joshi, Kireet (1999) in his article on fundamental duties and human values focused that values are important for the upliftment of human life. The author also discussed how various values such as justice, equality, liberty, fraternity, humanism, scientific temper, spirit of enquiry, protection of environment, love and compassion as well as the role of teacher towards helping students develop the art of practising values in concrete situations of life. The author suggested that the teachers should themselves be value oriented and enthusiastically participate in different programmes of value education.

Vaithilingam, M. (1999) studied the aspirations, values of children and fertility behaviour in rural Tamil Nadu. The study revealed that the educational aspirations of children both sons and daughters were high, however it was found moderate in case of professional aspiration. In both educational and professional aspirations a slight disparity was noticed between sons and daughters i.e. higher aspirations for sons than daughters. The study further revealed that high socio-economic status group gave preference to psychological values, whereas, poor socio-economic status group attached more importance to economic values.

Devi, B. (2000) made an analysis on the degradation of moral values among the youths of Manipur. The author tinted on various factors such as socio-religious factors, educational factors, the role played by media, family structure, alcohol, drugs and corruption that are responsible for the degradation of moral values amongst the youths of Manipur.

Kishore, L. (2000) in his article discussed about the need of incorporating value education in science teaching. The author stated that schools are not doing what needs to be done. The author also worried about non-implementation of recommendations of various commissions regarding value education. The value related concepts, their nature and classification were discussed in detail. The author suggested that the role and attitude of science teachers in value education must be positive and they should be able to resolve the value conflict of children and help them develop a scientific world view.

Islam, Sirajul (2002) in his study of value pattern of college students revealed that college students were mostly inclined towards modern values and attitudes. The study also revealed that BSc students endorsed modern progressive outlook in their values and attitudes than B.A. and B.Com students. The investigator has also reported a significant difference between high socio-economic status group and low socio-economic status group as well as high media exposure group and low media exposure group in relation to their values and attitudes.

Pamei, Shaganglung (2002) in his study of social motives, values and level of aspiration as related to identity crisis among Naga students found that Naga students strongly believe in a set of terminal and instrumental values. Their most preferred terminal values were salvation, wisdom while least preferred were true friendship. Again their most preferred instrumental values were honesty and ambition whereas least preferred value was forgiveness. The study further revealed that level of aspiration had significant effect on some of the Naga Problem Questionnaire items. Goal Discrepancy score had significant effect on five items, Attainment Discrepancy score had significant effect on three items, while Number of Times Goal Reach Score had significant effect on Two Naga Problem Items.

Pathak, M. (2002) in her investigation to study the impact of family environment, locus of control and level of aspiration upon achievement motivation of undergraduate students reported that the relationship between educational aspiration and achievement motivation was statistically insignificant. The researcher also revealed that male undergraduates were significantly higher on educational aspiration than their female counterparts.

Joshi, T. C. (2003) conducted a study to find out the social attitude, level of aspiration and scholastic achievement as predictors of self-confidence. The findings revealed that educational, personal, social i.e. the total aspiration was positively and significantly related with self-confidence of students. The study further revealed that among aspiration areas— educational, personal, social and total aspiration contributes 17.3 per cent, .6 per cent, 5.53 and 17.1 per cent respectively to self-confidence.

Bhatt, P. D. (2005) made a comparative study of sports persons with regard to their level of aspiration, self-confidence, risk-taking tendency and will to win. Comparisons were made on the basis of sex and type of sports. The research results revealed that sex had no role in creating educational as well as personal aspiration among sports person. Type of game did not account for increasing personal aspiration but girls playing group games had higher aspiration than boys playing group games. The findings further revealed that girl sports persons had significant high score than the boy sports persons with regard to social aspiration.

Fartiyal, P. (2005) investigated the home environment, level of aspiration and self-confidence as predictors of achievement motivation of professional and non-professional college students. The analysis of the result showed that personal and educational aspiration were significantly related and contributes to achievement motivation of professional college students. But the relationship between social aspiration and achievement motivation was found to be insignificant for college students. The study further concluded that total aspiration was not correlated with achievement motivation.

Vijayalakshmi, Ghali (2006) in her study on prioritisation of secondary school children's values by their parents and teachers, revealed that teachers and parents gave more importance to only five values, namely worthiness, sympathies, discipline, equality and caring. The results further revealed that hundred per cent of teachers gave priority to open mindedness, practicality, academic bent of mind, self-reliance, forgiveness, obedience and creativity, whereas hundred per cent of parents gave priority to the values namely honesty, truthfulness, cleanliness, duty mindedness, love, kindness, spirituality, humanity aesthetics morality, punctuality, cooperation and objectivity. Light difference ranging from 81 per cent to 97 per cent was observed in the preference of values of teachers and parents. The study reported a significant difference between rural and urban teachers as well as parents, male and female teachers as well as parents, educated and uneducated parents above 40 years, rich and poor parents and teachers teaching arts and science subjects with regard to values.

Simpson, Km. K. (2007) studied the socio-genetic needs, level of aspiration and self-concept as predictors of risk-taking behaviour among adolescents. The study reported that educational and social aspiration is positively correlated with risk-taking behaviour of adolescents. No significant correlation was observed between personal aspiration and risk-taking behaviour. The study concluded that, though level of aspiration was significantly related with risk taking behaviour, it did not account for generating this behaviour.

Tripathi, Sujit Ram (2008) conducted a study entitled "patterns of social identity and value orientation and their implications for conflict resolution". In this study the multiple regressions for conflict resolution styles indicated that values were more powerful predictors than social identities for conflict resolution. It further revealed that females and adults had higher scores on social and protection values while males and young adults were higher on personal and growth values.

Kauts and Kaur (2010) in their investigation on value preferences among adolescents revealed that common preferred values of boy and girl adolescents were world at peace, freedom, true friendship, wisdom, national security, equality, salvation, courageous, honesty, self-control, forgiving and cheerful. So far the terminal values were concerned, the study revealed that boys placed highest preference to value-wisdom and lowest preference to value-salvation, whereas these were the value of national integration and mature love respectively for girl adolescents. Again, with regard to instrumental values, the boys preferred honesty the most and cheerful the least, whereas these were honesty and logical respectively for girls.

Benjamin, B. Maxwell (2011) conducted a study to find out the prevalence of moral judgement among higher secondary school students of Chennai city with respect to classification of different school climate and home environment. The findings revealed that the school students in high school climate had higher moral, personal, social, aesthetic, humanitarian and religious values than the students in moderate and low school climate. On the other hand, in all these values the scores among the students of moderate and low school climates were similar. Contrary to this, the academic value was found similar among school students irrespective of the level of school climate. With regard to the influence of home environment, the study showed that in moral, personal, academic, social and aesthetic values students were similar irrespective of the level of home environment (high, moderate and low), whereas in humanitarian and religious values the students of low home environment were significantly higher than the students of high and moderate home environment.

Rajkumari, Sumati (2011) designed a cross-cultural study to examine the impact of home and school environment on values of adolescence girls of Coimbatore city of Tamil Nadu and Imphal West of Manipur. The results revealed that girls of Coimbatore city obtained higher mean scores for aesthetic, economic, family prestige and hedonistic values than their counterparts, whereas girls of Imphal West of Manipur obtained higher scores in religious, social, knowledge, power and health values. With respect to the impact of home environment, the study revealed that control and protective dimensions of home environment had positive correlation with religious and democratic values of the Coimbatore girls. So far the girls of Imphal West of Manipur were concerned the study found that permissiveness and religious value, rejection and knowledge value, deprivation of privilege with hedonistic, social and power values, protectiveness and democratic value; reward and knowledge value, permissiveness and hedonistic value were positively related.

Shagufta and Mariya (2012) argued that due to modern developments and fast changing role of parents, it has been very difficult for parents to inculcate significant values in their child and as such value oriented education needs to be realistically achievable in consonance with the academic framework of a school. The authors advocate that a judicious combination of academics, culture and value education will be an ideal approach to education and value education needs to be integrated within the school curriculum.

Sucharitha, R. (2012) conducted a study to examine the influence of seven independent variables namely sex, class of study, locality, subject of the study, level of institution, age and family size on moral judgement of secondary school students. The author revealed that sex and class of study had no significant influence on the moral judgement of secondary school students. However, the girl students scored higher in the mean score of moral judgement. The study further revealed existence of significant difference between rural and urban students in their moral judgement.

2.2. Studies Done Abroad

Arceneaux (1990) conducted a study on personality characteristics and values of 95 college students divided into three groups based on their achievement. He administered three measures to study their personality characteristics, interests and values. The study revealed that the three achievement groups differed consistently with the majority of differences involving socialisation or conformity. A gender difference was also noted in this regard.

Macneil (1990) investigated the relative importance of twenty values and their relationships with aspiration, life roles and work of 157 senior undergraduate students. The findings of the study showed that the respondents were inclined to value areas of personal intelligence, achievement and social orientation, and vocational aspirations. Statistically significant correlation was reported between values and career aspirations. The study further showed that the senior undergraduate students gave more importance to those values which emphasise social orientation and personal development.

Harbison (1991) conducted a study on value orientations and career aspirations of the students pursuing MSW degree at University of Toronto. A comparison was made between those entering into the MSW programme with a BSW degree and those entering without a BSW degree. The study indicated that those holding the BSW degree have different career expectations and aspirations than those who did not hold this degree. It was also reported that holding or not holding a BSW degree had no significant impact on respondent's value orientations. However, the result reported a relationship of value orientations with demographic characteristics and career aspirations.

Mendoza (1991) conducted his study on school personnel, students and parents of four single-sex catholic secondary schools. The study revealed that students' values, aspirations and self-esteem are nurtured through the care and respect received from teachers and parents. The study further concluded that the community of values in Catholic Church enable students, parents and school personnel to aspire and even achieve higher.

Menell (1991) conducted a study to explore and describe the values, level of satisfaction and aspiration of counselling psychology doctoral students. Nine women from three different counselling psychology doctoral programmes were participated in the study. A total of 21 semi-structured interviews were conducted. The findings revealed that the participants endorsed highest priority to practice oriented values such as introspection, connectedness in relationships and feelings over thinking. Thus, the result indicated that the participant did not perceive differences between their personal and professional values.

Basolene (1992) studied the aspirations and values of African and Asian theological students. Thirty eight students including nineteen from Africa and nineteen from Asia were sampled for interview. It was perceived by the students interviewed that, going on with their higher aspiration for education was the way to qualify for political, religious and socio-economic values.

Christensen (1992) reported significant sex differences in values as measured by the Rokeach value survey. He found that males ranked the values of loyalty and ambition higher than the females.

Kruezer, B. Katherine (1992) in his study on the effect of gender, gender-role orientation, socio-economic status and parental influence on women's aspirations stated that female have lower aspiration to leader and hope less in their career than do men.

Maddy (1992) made a post-positivist inquiry into the aspirations, values, motives and actions of women in senior level university leadership roles. The study indicated that upward mobility or career advancement is associated with a specific set of common values.

Smulders, A. E. M. (1995) made an attempt to explore the perceptions of private companies in Malaysia in 16 values as defined by the Ministry of Education. The findings revealed that all companies considered the values more desirable for supervisory workers than for non-supervisory workers. Eleven values out of 16 were found significantly more desirable for supervisory workers than for non-supervisory workers. The study further revealed that the domestic as well as foreign companies considered values with an interpersonal focus as less desirable and important than values with a personal focus (self-actualisation or competence values) with the exception of honesty.

Musek, J. (1998) conducted a study to explore whether the political and religious adherence of Slovenian students were substantially related to their individual values. The result of the investigation confirmed that political and religious adherence of Slovenian students was significantly connected to each other. The study further revealed that the group with different political notion differed clearly in the related importance of single value and common value category.

Bond, R., and Saunders, P. (1999) in their study on the factors influencing occupational attainment of British young males with different age levels, showed that at both age of 11 and 16 years, children's aspirations were positively related to their test scores. Thus, the findings implied that aspirations is influenced and raised by their academic ability.

Cyril, S. (1999) made a comparative study on educational and cultural determinants of values among adolescents of three countries i.e. England, Saudi Arabia and the United States. The results revealed significant differences among the adolescents of these three cultures; i.e. adolescents from England gave importance to parents and friendship, American adolescents gave importance to being well adjusted and feeling good about oneself and the prominence given to Islam by the Saudi Arabian adolescents.

Abu-Hilal, M. M. (2000) investigated the structure of attitudes to school subjects and the casual relationship among attitudes, levels of aspiration and achievement of 280 California high school students. The findings revealed that attitude to school indirectly influenced achievement, while aspiration significantly affected achievement and mediated between attitudes and achievement.

Schludermann, E. H. *et al.* (2000) reported no significant gender difference among adolescents in religiosity, social adjustment or personal adjustment. However, girls endorsed social values much more than boys did. The study further revealed that religiosity had much higher correlations with social values and social adjustment among boys than among girls.

Duane H. Bajema and others (2002) concluded that high school seniors lived in towns and farms had a high level of congruence between educational and occupational aspiration. They further perceived that farm and town students had equally diverse aspirations.

Ismael, Abu-Saad (2003) attempted to study the work values of Arab elementary school teachers in Israel in a multi-cultural context. Data was collected through using Islamic Work Ethic (IWE) and Work Individualism scales developed by Ali (1988). Based on the factor analysis of the IWE scale, the author revealed three factors of work value of Arab elementary teachers. These were (1) personal and organisational obligations; (2) personal investment and dividends; and (3) personal effort and achievement.

Schoon, I. (2006) in his/her work showed that young people from socially advantaged backgrounds endorsed higher aspirations than young people with socially disadvantaged background. The author further depicted a persisting gap in aspirations between the young people who experienced social adversity based on parental social status, home ownership, overcrowding and maternal education in their early childhood and those who did not.

Ferran *et al.* (2007) conducted a study of the relationship between the psychological wellbeing of Spanish adolescents from 12 to 16 years old and the values they aspire to for the future. The analysis of the results revealed that boys scored significantly higher on the materialistic value and the capacities and knowledge related value dimensions, while the girls scored higher on the interpersonal related value dimensions. The study further revealed that the youngest adolescents scored higher on materialistic values, while the oldest scored higher on interpersonal relationships related values.

Strand and Winston (2008) in their study on educational aspirations of inner city schools in Britain documented that aspiration of pupils was significantly influenced by their academic self-concept (i.e., the perception of one's academic abilities). The study further revealed that high aspirations of Black African and Asian groups possessed a strong academic self-concept, whereas the low aspirations of White British pupils tend to have a generally poor academic self-concept.

Gerdien D., Bertram Troost, Simone A. de Roos & Siebren, Miedema (2009) studied the role played by secondary schools on the development of the religious identity among the adolescents of Dutch Christian secondary schools. The findings of the result revealed a small relationship between the way the field of religious education is shaped in secondary education and the (actual) religious explorations and commitments of pupils. The authors showed that there was a much more direct relationship between pupils' religious explorations and commitments and their religious background, world view orientations and value orientations.

Rogers, Mary E. (2010) made a multivariate analysis of personality, values and professional and lifestyle expectations and well-being as correlates of career aspirations of 179 final year medical students. The researcher argued that understanding the expectations and values of this generation of doctors would assist workforce planners to address expected shortage and multi-distribution of practitioners.

Bobowi, Magdalena (2011) conducted a study on personality and parents' values as the predictors of students' personal values. The findings of the study revealed a greater contribution of multicultural personality to the variance in stimulation, self-direction, universalism and achievement values in comparison to the impact of parental values, whereas an opposite pattern was found for power, benevolence, and conformity. Furthermore, overall trait-like parents' values were better predictors of the offspring's trait-like values and the same effect held for parental societal values that predicted better the offspring's societal values.

Boxer, Paul and others (2011) revealed that students who aspire to achieve more than they expect to achieve are likely to have more economically disadvantaged backgrounds and poor academic performance. These students also reported lower level of school bonding, higher levels of test/performance anxiety and elevated behavioural/emotional difficulties.

Cochran, Daria B. (2011) reported that socio-economic status and ability influence the formation of aspirations (occupational) of adolescents.

Domene, Jose F. (2011) in his study on the effects of aspiration and career outcome expectation on academic motivation in post-secondary students concluded that compared to other post-secondary students, those with high aspiration and career expectation were more intrinsically and extrinsically motivated to academics.

Iglesias and Ricardo (2011) found differences in personal and interpersonal values across generational cohorts, gender and ethnic group. The study further revealed that male nurses are likely to take fewer risks and show a tendency towards congruence with the predominant organisational culture.

Lin, Meng-Jie (2011) assessed the effect of economic prospects, parental attitudes and gender values on female undergraduates' aspirations for masters and doctoral degree programmes in Taiwan's universalised and stratified higher education system. The study revealed that parental expectations and women's aspirations declined with educational level. They were higher for master's education and much lower for doctoral education. It was also found that specialisation and university ranking substantially affect women's aspirations for graduate education.

Julia, Ipgrave (2012) studied the relationships between local patterns of religious practice and young people's attitudes to the religiosity of their peers among secondary schools across the UK. The data indicated that students' respect for the religiosity of their peers was more influenced by the experience of religion in the neighbourhood and the degree to which being 'religious' is viewed as 'normal' there, rather than by the classroom Religious Education (multi-faith or otherwise).

Nataša, Pantiæ and Theo, Wubbels (2012) conducted a study on the role of teachers in inculcation of the moral values. The study was conducted to identify different conceptions on the teachers' moral roles so that an instrument can be developed which could assess the teachers' beliefs regarding those roles which in turn can be used in teacher development. By analysing the collected data, three moral roles of teachers were operationalised which were paternalist, liberal and social-relativist conceptions.

2.3. Trend Analysis of Related Literature

The foregoing account of the related literature generated in India as well as abroad has made the researcher clear that although a number of research studies have so far been conducted on values, still there is lacking of some areas specially related to level of aspiration in value dimensions of undergraduate students of professional courses.

So far the value dimensions of undergraduate students are concerned, it is evident from the review of related literature that, most of the studies conducted so far are on the students of conventional courses viz, Arts, Science and Commerce, whereas it is not adequately investigated targeting the students of professional courses. Except, Manav, Ram Niwas (1981), who conducted his study on attitudes, self-concept and values of professional and non-professional college students, no other study is reported so far to study the value dimensions of undergraduate students of professional courses at large. However, few specific areas of professional courses where studies are reported are *Medical Education* (Rogers, Mary E., 2010); *Teacher Education* (Khanna, Neeta, 1993); Business Studies (Narayanan, S.; Shantha Kumar, D. K.; Rao, K. S., and Kumar, K. G., 1994). Moreover, Dhekwar, T. M. (1996) has made a comparative study on personality traits and value pattern of students of technical and non-technical courses, but the study was conducted targeting the higher secondary students. Thus, no study is found to investigate the value dimensions of undergraduate students of professional courses at large.

A similar picture is observed with regard to level of aspiration also. Most of the studies conducted so far on level of aspiration aimed to identify its nature and relationship with variables like *Gender, Age, Area of Residence, Socio-Economic Status*, *Specialisation of Study* etc. *Gender* (Vaithilingam, M. 1999; Pathak, M. 2002; Bhatt. P. D. 2005); *Area of Residence* (Duane H. Bajema and others 2002); *Socio-Economic Status* (Schoon, I. 2006; Cochran, Daria, B. 2011); *Specialisation of Study* (Domene, Jose F., 2011). Few other studies revealed that aspiration is related to *academic traits of students* (Bond, R., and Saunders, P. 1999; Abu-Hilal, M. M. 2000; Domene, Jose F., 2011). So far the relationship of level of aspiration with value dimensions is concerned, the literature accounts very meagre. Only three studies undertaken by Macneil (1990), Basolene (1992), and Ranu, Sarbjit Kaur (1995), are found in this regard. Further analysis showed that none of the three studies aimed to investigate the relationship between level of aspiration and value dimensions of undergraduate students of professional courses.

It is to be noted that, though Manav, Ram Niwas (1981) conducted his study on value dimensions of undergraduate students involving a comparison between the students of professional and non-professional colleges, the study did not include level of aspiration as one of its variable as that of the present study does.

Moreover, the researcher could locate only two studies conducted in Assam investigating the value pattern of students. Islam, Sirajul (2002) examined the value pattern of college students in relation to socio-educational variables, whereas, Bhagawati, Binita (1999), made a comparative analysis of value orientation in two school system of Assam (Vidya Bharati system and General school system). Thus, the review of related literature is evident of the fact that no study has been done so far in Assam in particular and in India in general on the value dimensions and its relationship with level of aspiration of undergraduate students of professional courses involving a comparison between students of technical and non-technical course. Thus, it becomes quite conspicuous that still much remains to be done in this regard which warrants that the present study to be conducted. The study is first of its kind and as such is expected to fill the gap in this regard.

Chapter - 3

Methodology

Conducting objective research in social sciences has become very important in the present era due to ever increasing complexities in society and conflicting conclusions of different researchers in same variables. Every scientific research follows some kind of methods that are scientific in nature. Methodology in the context of the research refers to the overall approach to be adopted with respect to the population and sampling design, tools of data collection and techniques of treating data. It is a matter of fact, that though all research work is carried out with some methods, the validity and accuracy of the findings are dependent upon the deftness and accuracy of the methodology adopted. Therefore, adopting proper methodology is of utmost importance in the whole research process, more particularly in generalising the results. After stating the problem, reviewing the recent developments in the field, formulating the objectives and hypotheses, the researcher needs to prepare the plan of work which provides him/her the blueprint and directs the activity on desired line so as to reach the predefined goal with accuracy without losing labour. In short, the question of 'how' of research is answered by research methodology.

The main objective of the present investigation is to identify the level of aspiration and preferences of six value dimensions of undergraduate students of professional courses and to examine whether any relationship exists among them. A comparison between students of technical and non-technical professional courses is also attempted with regard to level of aspiration and value dimensions. As such the present chapter deals with the methods and procedure, identification of population, sampling technique and sample size, tools used for data collection and statistical techniques employed.

3.1. Method Used

The present study has been conducted under the descriptive method. This method is the most popular and widely used research method in social sciences and in education. It is that method of investigation which attempts to describe and interpret what exists at present in the form of conditions, practices, social units, trends, effects, attitudes, beliefs, some behaviour etc. It is concerned with the phenomena that are typical of the normal conditions. Descriptive research can also be sub-divided into several categories like Surveys, Case study, Genetic studies, Cross-Cultural studies, Correlational studies, Ex-Post Facto research etc. The present study is a descriptive correlational research. Descriptive correlational studies are those studies which try to test the hypotheses on relationship between two or more variables. Therefore, this method seemed to be most appropriate in the present investigation as it aims at a study of value dimensions of students and to study its relationship with level of aspiration.

3.2. Identification of the Population

Defining population is the primary requirement of any research work. It is difficult to adopt proper sampling procedure and select representative sample if the population is not well defined. The present study has aimed at a study on the value dimensions of undergraduate students of professional courses. It has been delimited to the undergraduate degree colleges of professional courses affiliated to Gauhati University which are 83 in count by the end of 2012, of which 16 are colleges of technical courses and 67 are colleges of non-technical professional courses. The study has excluded those conventional degree colleges which offer one or two professional subjects. As such the study has included all the students irrespective of sex and locality enrolled at undergraduate level in all the 83 degree colleges affiliated to Gauhati University offering education in professional courses during the study period of 2010 to 2013 as its population.

3.3. The Sampling Design

After defining the population, the most important task on the part of the researcher is to draw an adequate representative sample from the population. It is one of the most crucial steps the researcher faces. No research study can be carried out without taking samples as it is not always feasible to intervene and observe each unit of population under controlled conditions. The questions of time, money and energy come all the way. Sampling procedure reduces the dilemma in investigating entire population and makes the study feasible by selecting smaller representative samples from the entire population to draw out inferences and to generalise results for the entire population. David S. Fox (1969) remarks, *"It is not possible to collect data from every respondent relevant to our study, but only from some fractional part of the respondents. This process of selecting the fractional part is called sampling."* Thus, sample is a smaller representative proportion of the population, the selection of which requires careful planning and appropriate procedure to avoid any criticism of the findings. If the sampling technique is not proper, the result will be of no use.

In the present study sampling has been done at two levels as (A) Selection of sample colleges and (B) Selection of sample students.

(A) Selection of Sample Colleges

Stratified Random Sampling method has been employed in selecting the sample colleges. The present study has aimed at an investigation of the value dimensions of undergraduate students of professional courses involving a comparison between students of technical and non-technical professional courses. Again, it has been delimited to those degree colleges which are affiliated to Gauhati University offering professional courses at undergraduate level which are 83 in number of which 16 are colleges of technical professional courses and 67 are colleges of non-technical professional courses. In order to select the samples, the colleges are first divided into two homogenous 'strata' as 'colleges of technical professional courses' and 'colleges of non-technical professional courses'. Thereafter, 30 per cent of the colleges have been randomly selected from both the stratums as sample colleges for the present study. Thus, a total of 25 undergraduate colleges of professional courses (05 colleges of technical professional courses and 20 colleges of non-technical professional courses) have been taken as sample for the present study.

The following measures are taken in selecting the sample colleges:

(i) Though a huge discrepancy has been observed between the number of undergraduate degree colleges offering technical and non-technical professional courses affiliated to Gauhati University which are 16 and 67 in number respectively, randomisation has been done at proportionate value in order to get a fairly representation of the two types of colleges.

(ii) Values may differ among students perusing different course contents. In the present study the researcher has used the term 'Technical Professional Course' to mean those professional subjects or stream of study which are under the purview of AICTE. These are Engineering, Technology, Management, Architecture, Town Planning, Pharmacy, Applied Arts & Crafts, Hotel Management and Catering Technology; and 'Non-technical Professional Course' referred to all other professional subjects or stream of study like Medicine, Education, Law, Music etc., except those which are under the purview of AICTE. As a matter of fact, in the present investigation certain types of colleges has been found large in number and some others very meagre, e.g. in the category of the colleges of non-technical professional courses maximum number is of education (B.Ed.) and law (L.L.B). Colleges offering courses in medicine, physical education, art and music etc. are very less in nubber. As such, care has also been taken to include all types of colleges as far as possible to guarantee a more representation of the distribution.

(B) Selection of Sample Students

Since the study has included 'Gender' as one of the variable for analysis, stratified random sampling method has been followed for selection of sample students from each of the selected colleges. This technique is used as it ensures a representative and cross-section of the population (male and female) in the samples. Sampling frames are developed for each of the selected colleges separately with the strength of male and female undergraduate students. Applying proportionate allocation, five per cent of students from both stratums 'Male' and 'Female' has been taken from each of the colleges separately to guarantee a more representative distribution of students throughout the colleges. There are altogether 4143 students in five selected colleges of technical professional courses of which 2747 are male and 1396 are female. Similarly, there are 2850 students in 20 selected colleges of non-technical professional courses of which 1272 are male and 1568 are female. Taking five per cent from each of the stratum, the total sample for the present study consisted of 351 undergraduate students of professional courses of which 208 are students of technical professional courses (138 male and 70 female) and 143 are students of non-technical professional courses (64 male and 79 female).

The sample lay out is shown in Chart-1 and Figure-1.

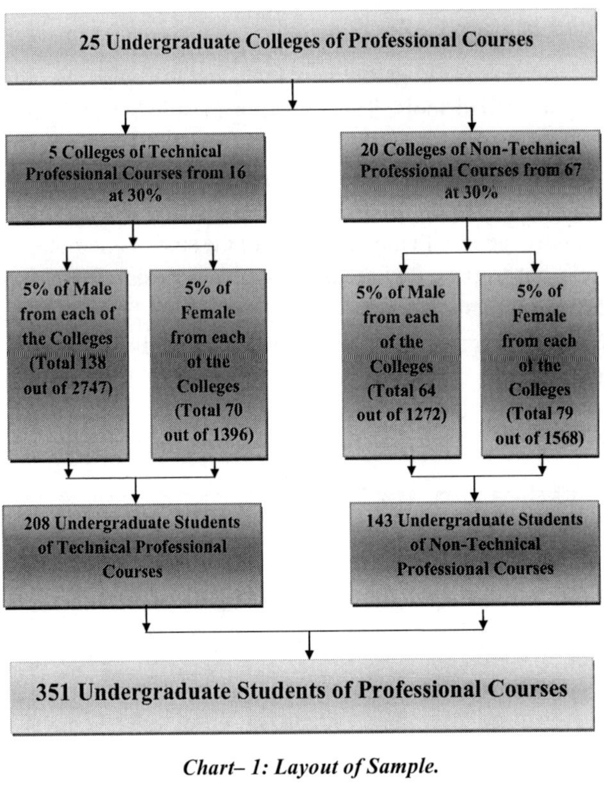

Chart– 1: Layout of Sample.

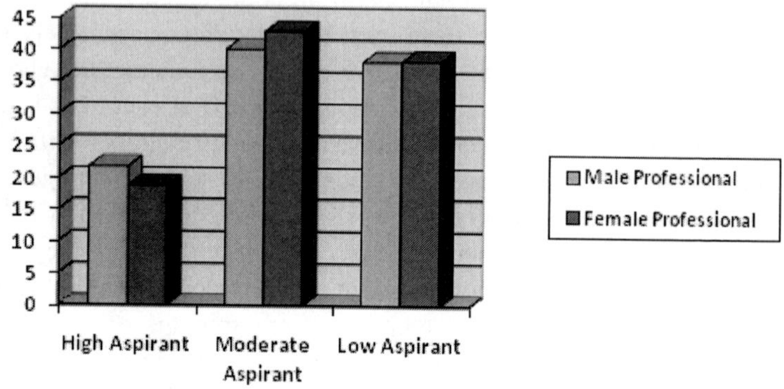

Figure-1: Graphical Representation of Course-wise and Gender-wise number of Samples taken for the study.

3.4. Tools of Data Collection

The instruments to gather new facts and to explore new fields in research are called tools. The selection of suitable tools is of vital importance for successful research work. While selecting the tools the researcher is to be very careful as tools should always reveal what the study intends to explore. In the present study also tools are selected in perfect consonance with the objectives of the study. Since, standardised tools relevant to the study are available, it is decided to use as such. The following standardised tools as shown in Table 3.1 has been employed considering the objectives of the study and feasibility of their use.

Table 3.1: Tools Used for the Study

Sl No.	*Name of the Tool*	*Variables Investigated*	*Contents of the Tool*	*Developed by*
1.	STUDY OF VALUES TEST (SVT)	Value Dimensions	Theoretical, Economic, Aesthetic, Social, Political and Religious	Dr. R. K. Ojha and Dr. Mahesh Bhargava
2.	LEVEL OF ASPIRATION MEASURE (LOA)	Level of Aspiration	Goal Discrepancy, Attainment Discrepancy and Number of Times Goal Reached	Dr. Mahesh Bhargava and Late Prof. M.A. Shah

Tool-1: Study of Values Test (SVT)

Description

The Study of Values Test is a standardised tool which measures the six basic interests or motives in personality of students studying in graduate and post-Graduate classes. These are Theoretical, Economic, Aesthetic, Social, Political and Religious. This type of classification is based upon Spranger's type(s) of men. Study of Values Test (SVT) has two parts. First part consists of 30 items with two alternative choices for each items and the second part consists of 15 items with four alternative choices for each item. In total, there are 45 statements with 120 alternative choices of which 20 alternative choices belong to each of the six values. Thus, each of the six value dimensions has an equal possibility of being scored in the scale (SVT).

Procedure of Administration and Scoring of Response of Study of Values Test (SVT)

The Study of Values Test is self-administering. It can be administered in group or individually. As the scale consists of two parts, it is necessary to give caution regarding the changes in alternative answers of Part-I and Part-II. In Part-I which consists of 30 items with two alternative answers each, the respondents need to assign score 2 and 1 or 3 and 0 to the two alternative answers according to his/her weightage of preference. Similarly in Part-II which includes 15 items with four alternative answers each, the respondents are to put scores as 4, 3, 2 and 1 according to the order of their most preference. As 20 alternative answers belong to each of the six value dimensions of which 10 alternatives belongs to Part-I and 10 belongs to Part-II, each value dimension has the probability of scoring a maximum of 70 and a minimum of 10 score.

The Study of Values Test is self-scoring also. It can be scored by the respondent himself or by the researcher. If any statement remains unanswered, then a score of 1.5 should be awarded to each alternative for Part-I and 2.5 to each alternative for Part-II. The rational is that each statement in Part-I carries a total of 3 score and each statement in Part-II carries a total of 10 score. Then, the vertical columns of scores in each page are to be added and entered in the boxes at the bottom of the page. Transcribing the total from each page in the space provided for the scoring table which is labelled with the same letter, one can get the scores on six value dimensions. The total score for the six columns gives the total score on values which must be equal to 240.

Validity and Reliability of Study of Values Test (SVT)

The Study of Values Test has been found to have content validity as revealed from the experts' views. The scale was administered to 500 male and 500 female graduate and post graduate students by the authors. The reliability of the scale was then determined separately for six value dimensions through using Split-half method which is presented in Table 3.2

Table 3.2: Reliability Coefficients of Study of Values Test (SVT)

Code	*Value dimensions*	*Reliability*
A	Theoretical	.78
B	Economic	.81
C	Aesthetic	.76
X	Social	.82
Y	Political	.83
Z	Religious	.84

Tool-2: Level of Aspiration Measure (LOA)

Description

Level of Aspiration Measure is a standardised tool designed by Dr. Mahesh Bhargava and Late Prof. M. A. Shah to measure the estimate of one's future expectation in a given task i.e. level of aspiration where the subject has to perform some activities. There are a total of eleven (11) performance sheet (including one practice trial sheet) which are arranged in the order of trial numbers 1 to 10. Each performance sheet contains 50 circles (each of 1 cm in diameter) which are arranged in five rows (ten circles in each row). Above and below the rows, there are two boxes on the right side. The upper box is for putting the number of expected score (except in practice trial) whereas the lower box is for writing the number of actual score or completed performance. Thus, ten trials are needed for each respondent besides practice trial.

Procedure of Administration and Scoring of the Performances of the Level of Aspiration Measure

This is a simple measure to administer upon any subject. It can be administered in group or individually. The respondents have a page containing 50 circles where he/she has to draw four lines so that they appear like a human face. The lines in the circles should be drawn in the sequence of Right Eye, Left Eye, Nose and Mouth. This activity has to perform for 30 seconds and after that the performer has to count the number of completed faces and enter it in the lower box labelled as actual score. This first trial is treated as practice trial where the respondents need not to put expected score before starting performance. In the proceeding trials, the respondents are to perform the same task along with putting the number of faces that he/she intends to complete within 30 second time duration on the basis of last actual performance in the upper box labelled as expected score. In this way the respondents need to complete 10 trials for actual work.

The scoring procedure of Level of Aspiration Measure is simple. It provides three types of scores: (a) Goal Discrepancy Score (GDS), (b) Attainment Discrepancy Score (ADS), and (c) Number of Times the Goal Reach Score (NTRS)

(a) Goal Discrepancy Score (GDS)

The extent and direction of the difference between actual score in the previous trial and expected score in the present trial is known as Goal Discrepancy Score, which is obtained by subtracting the actual score on a trial from the expected score for the next trial. Thus, if expected score on the next trial is higher than the actual score on the previous trial, the GDS is positive whereas if it is less than the actual score on the previous trial, the GDS will be negative. The extent and size of the discrepancy shows how high or low one sets the goal.

(b) Attainment Discrepancy Score

It is the difference between expected score (aspiration) and actual score (achievement) on the same trial and can be obtained by subtracting the expected performance from the actual performance on the same trial. The size of the discrepancy shows the extent to which one surpasses or fails to reach his goal.

(c) Number of Times the Goal Reach Score (NTRS)

This may be obtained by the number of times where the respondent's actual score is equal to or more than expected score. NTRS provides an index of respondent's actual probability of reaching his pre-determined goal.

In the present investigation, according to the suggestion of the author of the scale, only Goal Discrepancy Score (GDS) has been taken into consideration as it is the index of level of aspiration. ADS and NTRS are the indexes of one's goal reaching behaviour.

Validity and Reliability of Level of Aspiration Measure

Level of Aspiration is a standardised tool where validity coefficients and reliability are reported by the authors at satisfactory level. The Constructors of the scale argued that no measure of level of aspiration has made any mention of validity coefficient because the question of validity is not relevant to the study of level of aspiration. The question of validity is relevant when one behaviour is inferred from other behaviour indirectly. But here in case of level of aspiration, the respondent involves in actual task proposed by and the situation is by and large realistic for him/her. Still the developers had tried to find out the validity coefficients of aspirations as shown in table 3.3.

Table 3.3: Validity Coefficients of Level of Aspiration Measure

Sl. No.	*External Validity Criteria*	*N*	*GDS*	*ADS*
1.	Card Sorting Tray Tasks	30	.58	.52
2.	Ansari and Ansari: The L.A. Coding Test	60	.73	.68
3.	V. P. Bhargava: Level of Aspiration (Coding method)	60	.67	.62
4.	J.S. Grewal: Occupational Aspiration Scale	60	.76	.65
5.	Sharma and Gupta: Educational Aspiration Scale Form V	60	.48	.56
6.	Deo Mohan Projective Test of Achievement Motivation (n-ach) Male Group Deo Mohan Projective Test of Achievement Motivation (n-ach) Female Group	4040	.72.78	.67.73
7.	T.R. Sharma: Academic Achievement Motivation Test (AAMT)	80	.84	.76

Note: N-Number of Cases, GDS- Goal Discrepancy Score, ADS-Attainment Discrepancy Score.

Again, the reliability of this measure is calculated by the measure developers through employing test-retest method and split-half method as shown in Table 3.4.

Table 3.4: Reliability Coefficients of Level of Aspiration Measure

Method	*N*	*Reliability*		
		GDS	*ADS*	*NTRS*
Test-retest Method				
With a gap of 1 month	100	.88	.82	.86
With a gap of 3 months	60	.72	.72	.74
Split Half Method	60	.77	.69	.78

3.5. Variables of the Study

Any scientific study aims to investigate the cause and effect relationship between two or more phenomena or variables. A concept which can take on different quantitative values is called a variable. Variables are the phenomenon or attributes through which the investigation proceeds in any scientific study. When a variable depends upon or is consequence of another variable it is termed as dependent variable and the variable that is antecedent to the dependent variable is termed as independent variable. In other words independent variable stands for the cause and dependent variable stands for the effect. Independent variables that are not related to the purpose of the study, but may affect the dependent variable are called extraneous variable (Kothari, C.R. 2008).

In the present investigation the six value dimensions namely, theoretical economic, political, social, aesthetic and religious are regarded as dependent variables and level of aspiration, sex and type of course (education) are treated as independent variables.

3.6. Collection of Data

The researcher himself has collected all the relevant data from all the sample students under consideration. In order to administer the tools, the investigator personally visited the selected degree colleges to appraise the authorities about the objectives of the study and to get permission to administer the tools. Then the complete list of students enrolled in different professional courses during the particular study period has been collected and the sampling frame is prepared accordingly. A tentative schedule has been finalised with the college authorities to administer the tools upon the students. Accordingly, the investigator met the students and was introduced to them by college authorities. Thereafter, the investigator has created rapport with the students and requested their cooperation through explaining the nature and objectives of the investigation. Both the tools are administered individually or in group of maximum 10 students at a time as both the tools adopted for the study do have the provision of both type of administration. In some cases after preparing the sampling frame the students are personally approached in hostels or residences and data have been collected accordingly. Before administering the tools a briefing of the test and instructions is made to the respondents' and ensured that they are at ease. While administering the Study of Values Test, efforts are made to explain that it is not a test of intelligence, skills or any kind of knowledge, but it is a test of personality only. Stop watch is used to count the time duration of 30 seconds in each trial of Level of Aspiration Measure. After collecting the data the respondents are thanked for their cooperation. In this way a day or two, has been spend in each sample colleges. The same agenda has been followed to collect data from all the sampled colleges.

3.7. Treatment of Data

The data that have been gathered for the present study is of quantitative type. Hence, only quantitative approach of treating data has been used in the present context. Quantitative approach is a set of numerical observation obtained as a result of counting or measuring some characteristics. As the present study is mainly based on examining group performances and relationship between variables, the statistical techniques employed for the study are 'frequency', 'percentage', 'mean', 'sd', 't-test', 'correlation', and 'regression-prediction' which are explained below in brief. The whole analysis is made through using *Statistical Package for Social Sciences (SPSS)* software.

1. Mean scores of all the six value dimensions as well as of level of aspiration has been computed for the entire group as well

as separately for the sub-groups. The preference order of value dimensions is determined on the basis of weightage of mean scores of the value dimensions for different groups. Again, to account the high, moderate and low aspirant students, the procedure of highest 33 per cent, middle 34 per cent and lowest 33 per cent of scores on level of aspiration has been employed as per the suggestion and advice of the authors of the scale Level of Aspiration Measure (LOA). In this way the frequencies of high, moderate and low aspirant students are calculated for all the categories, viz. undergraduate students of technical and non-technical professional courses, male and female undergraduate students of professional courses, male and female undergraduate students of technical as well as non-technical professional courses.

2. The t-test has been applied to determine the significance of difference in the mean scores of six value dimensions as well as level of aspiration score between male and female students of technical and non-technical professional courses.
3. Pearson's correlation technique has been used to examine the relationship between scores of level of aspiration and each of the six value dimensions of Study of Values Test (SVT).
4. The t-test (CR) has been used to determine the significance of difference in the relationship of level of aspiration and each of the six values of Study of Values Test (SVT) between various groups.
5. Linear regression coefficients has been computed and regression equations of level of aspiration (predictor variable) on each of the six value dimensions (criterion variables) are set up separately for students of technical and non-technical professional courses, male and female students of professional courses, male and female students of technical as well as non-technical professional courses and students of professional courses as a whole. Furthermore, Coefficients of Forecasting Efficiency for each of the Regression Equations are calculated and presented in per cent to understand the efficiency level of level of aspiration in predicting value dimensions.

The .05 level of confidence interval has been adopted to determine the statistical significance of 't' value, 'r' value and 'CR' value in all cases.

3.8. Delimitation of the Study

The present study has been delimited to the undergraduate students of degree colleges affiliated to Gauhati University offering education only in professional courses.

A brief glance of the research design is presented in chart 2 as below.

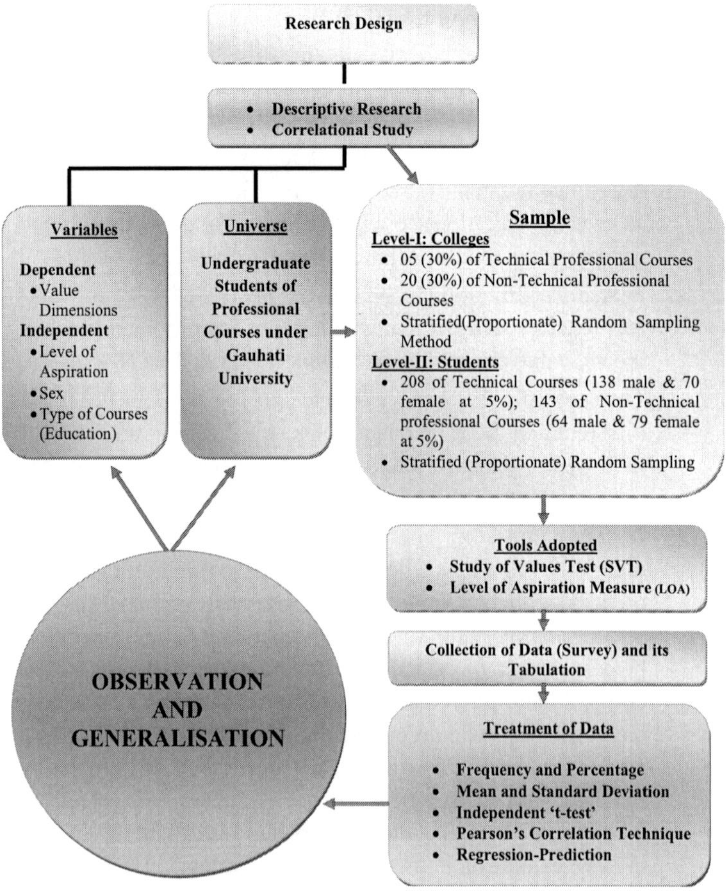

Chart 2: Flow Chart of the Research Design.

Chapter - 4

Analysis and Interpretation of Data

In order to answer the research questions, a systematic analysis of data is the most essential part of any scientific research. Data analysis means studying the collected material from as many angles as possible to discover the inherent facts. The Present chapter deals with the same. The data that are being gathered for the present study is of quantitative type. Hence, only quantitative approach of treating data has been used in present context. Quantitative approach is a set of numerical observations obtained as a result of counting or measuring some characteristics. As the present study is mainly based on examining group performances and relationship between variables, the collected data are carefully and systematically processed and analysed through employing most suitable statistical techniques like mean, standard deviation, t-test, Pearson's correlation test, regression-prediction etc. according to the detailed procedures described in Chapter-III. The whole analysis has been made through using Statistical Package for Social Sciences (SPSS) software.

In order to have a bird's eye view of the results of the study, the data have been analysed and presented in the order of the objectives of the study.

Objective-1: ***To study the value preferences of undergraduate students of both technical and non-technical professional courses of Gauhati University.***

In order to answer the first objective, the mean scores and standard deviations of different value dimensions are calculated separately for the undergraduate students of technical and non-technical professional courses. As all the six dimensions of values have equal chances of scoring, hence, preference order has been assigned to each of the value dimensions according to the weightage of respective mean scores separately for the two groups, which are presented in Table 4.1. The mean scores of both the groups in different value dimensions are also graphically presented through Figure 2.

Table 4.1: Mean scores and Preference order of Value Dimensions of Undergraduate Students of both Technical and Non-Technical Professional Courses

Value Dimensions	*Students of Technical Professional Courses (N=208)*			*Students of Non-Technical Professional Courses (N=143)*		
	Mean	*SD*	*Preferences*	*Mean*	*SD*	*Preferences*
Theoretical	45.00	5.939	I	42.83	4.716	II
Economic	44.38	6.110	II	42.90	6.080	I
Social	38.03	5.766	IV	39.48	6.074	IV
Political	39.76	5.074	III	40.33	4.927	III
Aesthetic	37.62	6.178	V	38.31	5.317	V
Religious	35.22	7.551	VI	35.99	6.110	VI

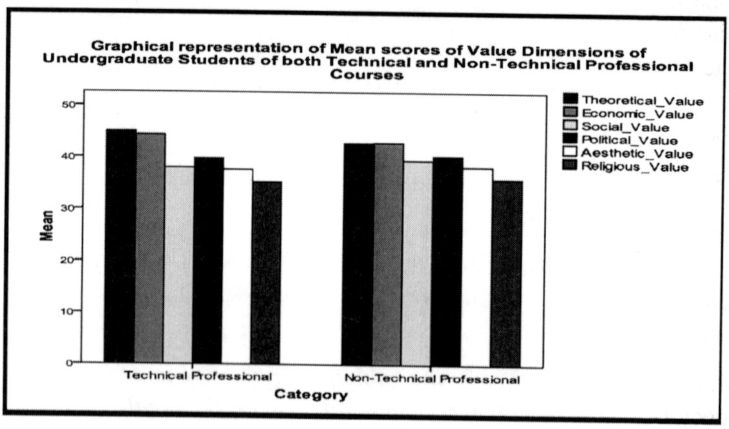

Figure-2:

The Table 4.1 shows that the preference order of value dimensions of undergraduate students of technical professional courses is theoretical, followed by economic, political, social, aesthetic and religious with mean scores of 45.00, 44.38. 39.76, 38.03, 37.62 and 35.22 respectively which is economic followed by theoretical, political, social, aesthetic and religious with mean scores of 42.90, 42.83, 40.33, 39.48, 38.31 and 35.99 respectively for students of non-technical professional courses. Thus, the mean scores of value dimensions reveal prominent variance between undergraduate students of technical and non-technical professional courses with regard to the two most preferred value dimensions. These are theoretical followed by economic value for students of technical professional courses, which has reversed for the students of non-technical professional courses. The preference order of remaining four dimensions under consideration remains same for the two groups, which is political followed by social, aesthetic and religious.

It is a fact that a theoretical man is critical and rational enough whereas an economic man gives more importance to utility. The two most preferred value dimensions of both the groups as theoretical and economic as found in Table 4.1 is not surprising at all. Higher importance on theoretical value by both the group of students seems to be the logical consequences of their being students of higher education. Being the students of undergraduate classes, they are expected to be critical and rational in nature, which are the characteristics of theoretical value. Similarly, placing more importance on economic value seems to be the effect of their being students of professional courses. Again, the preference of theoretical value over economic value by students of technical professional courses and preference of economic value over theoretical value by students of non-technical professional courses is perhaps because of the nature of education that they are being exposed.

The third and fourth preferred value of the both technical and non-technical professional course students are political and social respectively, implying that irrespective of nature of course-contents, the undergraduate students of professional courses are political or power motivated than being social, co-operative, sympathetic and helpful.

It is also not surprising to see that the two least preferred values of both the groups are aesthetic followed by religious. Since, economic and theoretical values are given more importance by the respondents; it is natural that they give less importance to aesthetic and religious value. The religious and aesthetic values are diametrically opposed to theoretical and economic value. The religious man is mystical and seeks to comprehend the cosmos as a whole by withdrawing from life which a theoretical man may not. Again, a religious man may not lust for wealth, luxury etc. which are the characteristics of an economic man. Similarly, an aesthetic person is imaginary and looks for diversity, where-as a theoretical man is critical, rational and looks for identity of experiences. Thus, in the pertinent, it can be said that the result of the Table 4.1 reveals what we generally observe in society.

Some of the previous research evidences with regard to value dimensions, though yielded contradictory results, yet most of them largely supports the results of the present study. The two most preferred values in the present study have been found theoretical and economic. The results of similar kinds were reported by Macneil (1990), Singh, Iqbal (1993), Ranu, Sarbjit Kaur (1995), Ravindranathan, M.N. (1997), and Sahoo, K.C., Biswal, A. and Khandai, H. (1998). Macneil (1990) showed that senior undergraduate students were more inclined to personal intelligence. According to Singh, Iqbal (1993) and Ranu, Sarbjit Kaur (1995), the second most preferred value of students was theoretical. Similarly, Ravindranathan, M.N. (1997) in his study showed that primary school teachers were more modern in their attitude towards educational and economic aspects of life, just as Sahoo, K.C., Biswal, A. and Khandai, H. (1998) reported that scientific value was high among university students. Again, the result of the present study that aesthetic and religious values are the two least preferred values of undergraduate students of professional courses also resembles with that of the result reported by Chuttaura, P. (1992), Kaur, Amarjeet (1993), Singh, Iqbal (1993), Ranu, Sarbjit Kaur (1995), Dhekwar, T.M. (1996) and Kauts and Kaur's (2010). Chuttaura, P (1992) and Ranu, Sarbjit Kaur (1995) found that the second least preferred value of the subject was aesthetic. Similarly, Kaur, Amarjeet, (1993), Singh, Iqbal (1993), Ranu, Sarbjit Kaur (1995), all have revealed that the least preferred value of the students was religious. According to Dhekwar, T.M. (1996) religious and aesthetic values were held at low position by students of both non-technical and technical-vocational course. Kauts and Kaur's (2010) revealed that the lowest preferred terminal value of adolescent boys was salvation which is influenced by religiosity.

The investigator has also intended to study gender-wise value preferences of undergraduate students of professional courses. Therefore, the mean scores and preference order of different value dimensions of both male and female undergraduate students of professional courses are determined and presented in Table 4.2. The mean scores of both the gender group in different value dimensions are also graphically represented through Figure 3.

Table 4.2: Mean scores and Ranking order of Value Dimensions of Male and Female Undergraduate Students of Professional Courses.

Value Dimensions	*Male Students of Professional Courses (N=202)*			*Female Students of Professional Courses (N=149)*		
	Mean	*SD*	*Preferences*	*Mean*	*SD*	*Preferences*
Theoretical	44.21	5.845	II	43.98	5.192	I
Economic	44.57	6.063	I	42.69	6.077	II
Social	38.07	6.304	IV	39.37	5.306	IV
Political	41.06	4.817	III	38.54	4.929	V
Aesthetic	36.61	5.739	V	39.65	5.541	III
Religious	35.46	7.334	VI	35.64	6.546	VI

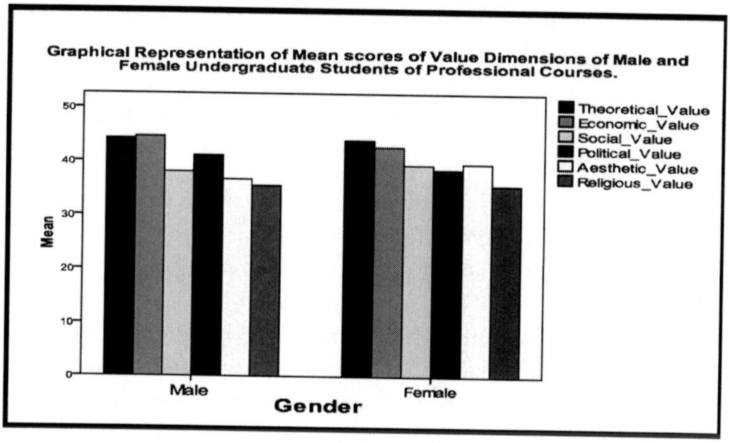

Figure-3

The result presented in Table 4.2 reveals that the order of preference of value dimensions of male students of professional courses is economic followed by theoretical, political, social, aesthetic and religious with mean scores of 44.57, 44.21, 41.06, 38.07, 36.61 and 35.46 respectively whereas this order is theoretical followed by economic, aesthetic, social, political and religious with mean scores of 43.98, 42.69, 39.65, 39.37, 38.54 and 35.64 respectively for the female counterparts. Thus, divergence is observed in the two most preferred values as well as third and fifth preferred values between male and female undergraduate students of professional courses. It is noted that the most preferred value of male group is economic, whereas with respect of female group it is theoretical. So far the second most preferred value is concerned, this order has changed. Theoretical is the second preferred value of male group and economic is that of the female group. Similar case is observed with regard to the third and fifth preferred value dimensions between male and female students. Political and economic values are ranked at third and fifth position by male group, whereas this order has changed in case of female group. However, the two groups i.e. male and female students of professional courses show complete identity in the preference order of the remaining two value dimensions i.e. social and religious. Both the groups placed social and religious value at fifth and sixth position respectively.

The inference of the findings of the Table 4.2 is that male undergraduate students of professional courses tend to be more utility oriented and practical in nature than being critical and theoretical as evident. Similarly, the preference of theoretical value over economic value by female students suggests that females are more critical and rational in nature than being utility oriented.

In order to have an in-depth understanding of the value pattern of the undergraduate students of professional courses, the investigator has also intended to study gender-wise value preferences of undergraduate students of both technical and non-technical professional courses separately. The mean scores and preference order of different value dimensions of male and female undergraduate students of technical professional courses are calculated and presented in Table 4.3. The result is also graphically represented through Figure 4.

Table 4.3: Mean scores and Preference order of Value Dimensions of Male and Female Undergraduate Students of Technical Professional Courses.

Value Dimensions	*Male Students of Technical Professional Courses (N=138)*			*Female Students of Technical Professional Courses (N=70)*		
	Mean	*SD*	*Preferences*	*Mean*	*SD*	*Preferences*
Theoretical	45.03	6.104	I	44.94	5.644	I
Economic	44.73	6.056	II	43.67	6.197	II
Social	37.75	5.826	IV	38.57	5.648	IV
Political	40.43	4.845	III	38.44	5.288	V
Aesthetic	36.93	6.077	V	39.00	6.188	III
Religious	35.15	7.873	VI	35.36	6.926	VI

Graphical Representation of Mean scores of Value Dimensions of Male and Female Undergraduate Students of Technical Professional Courses

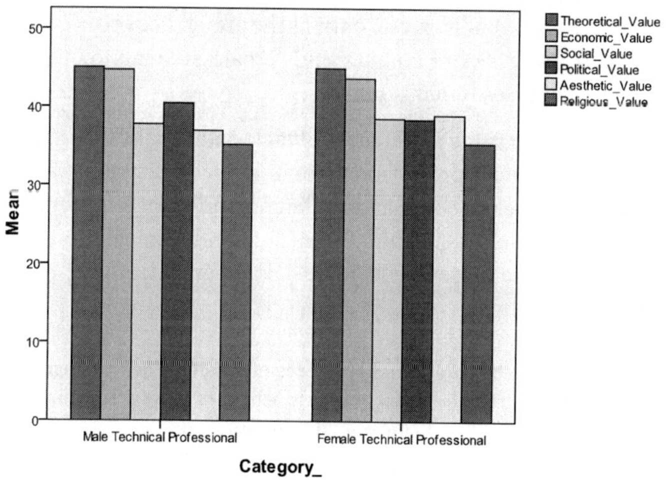

Figure-4

The perusal of the result depicted in Table 4.3 reveals that the order of preference of value dimensions of male students of technical professional courses is theoretical followed by economic, political, social, aesthetic and religious with mean scores of 45.03, 44.73, 40.43, 37.75, 36.93 and 35.15 respectively whereas this order is theoretical followed by economic, aesthetic, social, political and religious with mean scores of 44.94, 43.67, 39.00, 38.57, 38.44 and 35.36 respectively for their female counterparts. Thus, divergence is observed in the third and fifth preferred values between the male and female undergraduate students of technical professional courses which are political and aesthetic respectively for the male group, whereas these are found reverse in case of female group. It is here to be noted that the order of preference of value dimensions of female undergraduate students of technical professional courses is found entirely similar to that of the order of value preference of female group of professional courses as a whole. Variance is observed in case of male group with regard to the two most preferred value dimensions which are economic followed by theoretical for males of professional courses as a whole, whereas these are reverse in case of male students of technical professional courses. Thus, it can be said that a change in the courses of study can cause a change in the order of two most preferred values i.e. theoretical and economic in case of male group only, as the preference order of female students of professional courses and female students of technical professional courses remains same.

Similar to the value preferences of male and female undergraduate students of technical professional courses, the investigator has also calculated the mean scores and preference order of different value dimensions of male and female students of non-technical professional courses, which are presented in Table 4.4 and graphically represented through Figure 5.

Table 4.4: Mean scores and Preference order of Value Dimensions of Male and Female Undergraduate Students of Non-Technical Professional Courses.

Value Dimensions	*Male Students of Non-Technical Professional Courses (N=64)*			*Female Students of Non-Technical Professional Courses (N=79)*		
	Mean	***SD***	***Preferences***	***Mean***	***SD***	***Preferences***
Theoretical	42.45	4.837	**II**	43.13	4.625	**I**
Economic	44.23	6.112	**I**	41.82	5.872	**II**
Social	38.75	7.233	**IV**	40.08	4.911	**IV**
Political	42.42	4.500	**III**	38.63	4.619	**V**
Aesthetic	35.94	4.908	**VI**	40.23	4.865	**III**
Religious	36.11	6.014	**V**	35.89	6.224	**VI**

Graphical Representation of Mean scores of Value Dimensions of Male and Female Undergraduate Students of Non-Technical Professional Courses.

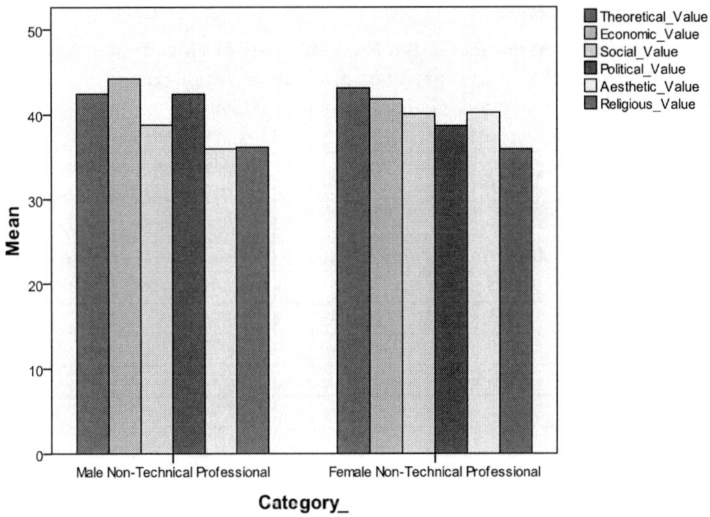

Figure-5

The result depicted in Table 4.4 reveals that the order of preference of value dimensions of male students of non-technical professional courses is economic followed by theoretical, political, social, religious and aesthetic with mean scores of 44.23, 42.45, 42.42, 38.75, 36.11 and 35.94 respectively whereas this order is theoretical followed by economic, aesthetic, social, political and religious with mean scores of 43.13, 41.82, 40.23, 40.08, 38.63 and 35.89 respectively for the female counterparts. Thus, maximum divergence is observed in the preference order of value dimensions between male and female undergraduate students of non-technical professional courses. Except the social value that is placed at fourth position by both male and female group, the rank order of other five values changed between the two groups.

As the study involves a comparison on value dimensions between undergraduate students of technical and non-technical professional courses, the researcher has tried to present the mean scores and also the preference order of different value dimensions of male undergraduate students of technical and non-technical professional courses together in Table 4.5 and through Figure 6 as below.

Table 4.5: Mean scores and Ranking order of Value Dimensions of Male Undergraduate Students of Technical and Non-Technical Professional Courses

Value Dimensions	*Male Students of Technical Professional Courses (N=138)*			*Male Students of Non-Technical Professional Courses (N=64)*		
	Mean	*SD*	*Preferences*	*Mean*	*SD*	*Preferences*
Theoretical	45.03	6.104	I	42.45	4.837	II
Economic	44.73	6.056	II	44.23	6.112	I
Social	37.75	5.826	IV	38.75	7.233	IV
Political	40.43	4.845	III	42.42	4.500	III
Aesthetic	36.93	6.077	V	35.94	4.908	VI
Religious	35.15	7.873	VI	36.11	6.014	V

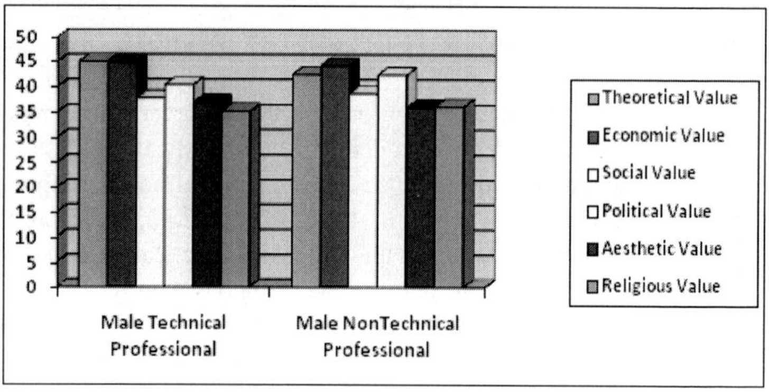

Figure 6: Graphical Representation of Mean Scores of Value Dimensions of Male Undergraduate Students of Technical and Non-Technical Professional Courses.

The preference order of value dimensions of male undergraduate students of technical professional courses is theoretical followed by economic, political, social, aesthetic and religious with mean scores of 45.03, 44.73, 40.43, 37.75, 36.93 and 35.15 respectively whereas this order is economic followed by theoretical, political, social, religious and aesthetic with mean scores of 44.23, 42.45, 42.42, 38.75, 36.11 and 35.94 respectively for the male undergraduates of non-technical professional courses as evident in the result depicted in table 4.5. Thus, divergence is observed in the two most as well as two least preferred value dimensions between the two groups. Theoretical and economic values are ranked at first and second position respectively by males of technical professional courses, while the male of non-technical professional courses put economic value first and theoretical value at second position. Similar case is observed with regard to aesthetic and religious values. Aesthetic and religious values are given fifth and sixth preference respectively by male undergraduates of technical professional courses, whereas this order has reversed in case of male of non-technical professional courses. Political and social values are given third and fourth preference respectively by both the groups.

The mean scores and preference order of different value dimensions of female undergraduate students of technical and non-technical professional courses are also presented together in Table 4.6 and through Figure 7 as below.

Table 4.6: Mean scores and Ranking order of Value Dimensions of Female Undergraduate Students of Technical and Non-technical Professional Courses

Value Dimensions	*Female Students of Technical Professional Courses (N=70)*			*Female Students of Non-Technical Professional Courses (N=79)*		
	Mean	*SD*	*Preferences*	*Mean*	*SD*	*Preferences*
Theoretical	44.94	5.644	I	43.13	4.625	I
Economic	43.67	6.197	II	41.82	5.872	II
Social	38.57	5.648	IV	40.08	4.911	IV
Political	38.44	5.288	V	38.63	4.619	V
Aesthetic	39.00	6.188	III	40.23	4.865	III
Religious	35.36	6.926	VI	35.89	6.224	VI

The result presented in Table 4.6 reveals that the order of preference of value dimensions of female undergraduate students of both technical and non-technical professional courses is theoretical followed by economic, aesthetic, social, political and religious with mean scores of 44.94, 43.67, 39.00, 38.57, 38.44 and 35.36 respectively for former

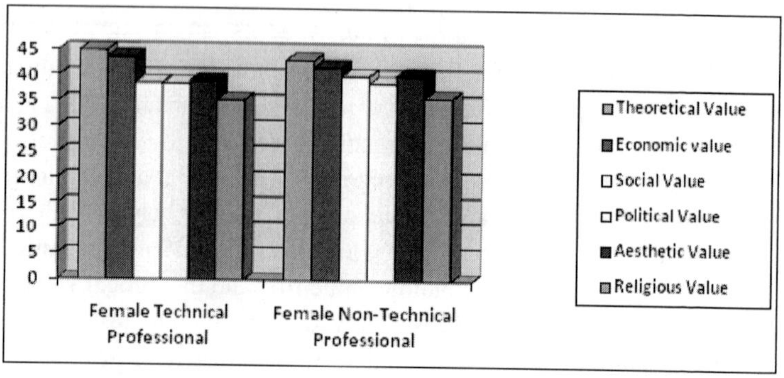

Figure 7: Graphical Representation of Mean Scores of Value Dimensions of Female Undergraduate Students of Technical and Non-Technical Professional Courses.

group and 43.13, 41.82, 40.23, 40.08, 38.63 and 35.89 respectively for later group. Thus, no variance is observed in the value preferences between female undergraduates of technical and non-technical professional courses. Here, it is also to be focused that the preference order of value dimensions of female undergraduate students of both technical as well as non-technical professional courses remains same as that of the female students of professional courses as a whole. This implies that any variance or change in nature of course does not accompany any change or variance in the value preferences so far the female undergraduate students of professional courses are concerned.

The investigator has calculated the mean scores and also the preference order of different value dimensions of undergraduate students of professional courses as a whole, which are presented in Table 4.7 and graphically represented through Figure 8 as below.

Table 4.7: Mean scores and Preference order of Value Dimensions of Undergraduate Students of Professional Courses

Value Dimensions	*Undergraduate Students of Professional Courses (N=351)*		
	Mean	***SD***	***Preferences***
Theoretical	44.11	5.571	I
Economic	43.77	6.132	II
Social	38.62	5.928	VI
Political	39.99	5.015	III
Aesthetic	37.90	5.844	V
Religious	35.53	7.001	VI

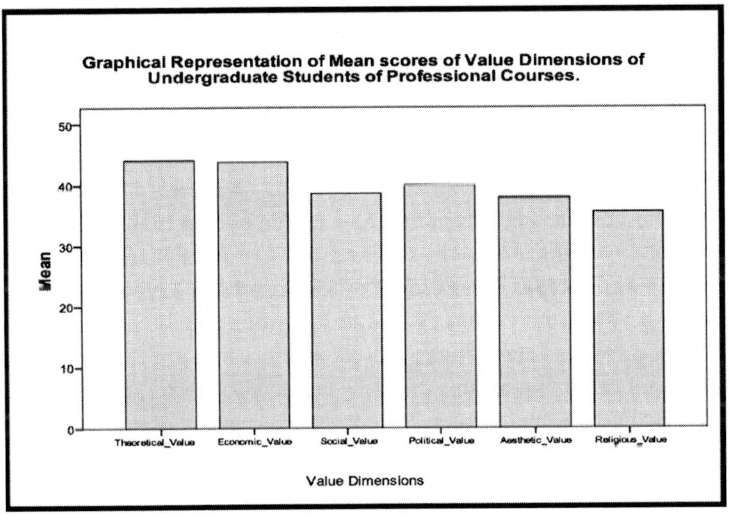

Figure-8

The perusal of the result presented in Table 4.7 reveals that the order of preference of value dimensions of undergraduate students of professional courses is theoretical followed by economic, political, social, aesthetic and religious with mean scores of 44.11, 43.77, 39.99, 38.62, 37.901 and 35.53 respectively. Thus, it can be inferred that undergraduate students of professional courses in general tend to be more critical and rational in nature than being utility oriented and practical in nature. Similarly, the preference of political value over social value implies that they are more interested in power and influence than being helpful, cooperative and kind hearted. Since their two most preferred values are theoretical and economic, it is natural that their least preferred values would be aesthetic and religious which are placed at fifth and sixth position respectively. Those who are fascinated to intellectual perfection and material wealth are likely to be unenthusiastic towards religious mystery as well as form and harmony. Thus, the result presented above fully or partly adheres to our general observations.

The foregoing analysis presented from Table 4.1 to Table 4.7 concentrates on the mean scores and preference order of value dimensions of the sample constituted sex-wise and course-wise. The results reveal that the most preferred value dimension of undergraduate students of professional courses is theoretical followed by economic. Political and social values are given third and fourth position respectively. And their least preferred value is religious followed by aesthetic.

The course-wise as well as sex-wise analysis reveals almost similar results. A minute analysis of the value preferences of male and female students of technical as well as non-technical professional courses also shows similar types of results. The results related to the preference order of value dimensions of all the sub-groups under consideration has revealed that theoretical and economic value are the two most preferred value dimensions of all the target groups irrespective of the nature of course and gender. Except the male group of non-technical professional courses who placed theoretical value at second place just after economic value, the other groups namely, male and female undergraduates of technical professional courses and female group of non-technical professional courses placed theoretical and economic value at first and second position respectively.

Irrespective of type of course and gender, the least preferred value of almost all the target groups is found religious, except the male group of non-technical professional courses. Since, theoretical and economic values are given more importance by the respondents; it is natural that they give less importance to religious value. The religious value is diametrically opposed to theoretical and economic value. The religious man is mystical and seeks to comprehend the cosmos as a whole by withdrawing from life which a theoretical man may not. Again, a religious man may not lust for wealth, luxury etc. which are the characteristics of an economic man.

Similarly, the social value is given relatively lower rank i.e. fourth position by all the target groups irrespective of nature of course and gender. This implies that irrespective of nature of course and gender, the undergraduate students of professional courses are relatively less social or co-operative, sympathetic and helpful. This is perhaps because they are being polished to become better professionals in different fields through their education system itself. Moreover, they are living in an age of competition and unemployment, where everybody tries to soar high in the sky through enhancing their own materialistic condition even at the cost of others. There is an unhealthy competition behind material gain among the members of society. Nurturing in such an environment, it is not surprising that the students of professional courses give less importance to social value and high to economic value.

It is notable to see that the preference order of value dimensions of female group of all category i.e. total samples of professional courses, samples of technical professional courses as well as non-technical professional courses remains same. This order is theoretical followed by economic, aesthetic, social, political and religious; implying that nature of course may not affect the value preference of female undergraduate students of professional courses. Provided that females of all types of courses give third preference to aesthetic value and fifth preference to political value, where as males of all types of courses give third preference to political value. That means females are more enthused in aesthetic pursuits than being political and motivated to power which the males do, rather they are more interested in *form and harmony*. Females find chief interest in the artistic episodes of life and try to enjoy each single impression for its own sake as evident, perhaps owing to the cultural stereotype of females being graceful, loving, kind and emotional. Male students are found more political than being aesthetic perhaps because of the stereotype of man leading and man dominated system and higher expectations of society and family. Thus, the findings regarding the nature of value dimensions among male and female undergraduate students of professional courses can be amply justified as quite valid and reliable.

Objective-2: *To examine whether there is significant difference between undergraduate students of technical and non-technical professional courses in their value dimensions.*

Ho_1: *There is no significant difference between undergraduate students of technical and non-technical professional courses in their value dimensions.*

In order to answer the second objective, 't- analysis' has been employed on the mean scores of each of the six value dimensions between the undergraduate students of technical and non-technical professional courses. Because, the stratified random sampling method is employed in drawing the samples, the use of 't-test' is amply justified, as stratified random samples ensure true representative of the population. Table 4.8 highlights the result of 't-analysis' on value dimensions between undergraduate students of technical and non-technical professional courses, where .05 level of confidence interval is taken into consideration.

Table 4.8: Significance of Difference between Mean Scores of Undergraduate Students of Technical and Non-Technical Professional Courses in each of the Six Value Dimensions.

Value Dimensions	*Students of Technical Professional Courses (N=208)*			*Students of Non-Technical Professional Courses (N=143)*			*t-value*	*Status*
	Mean	*SD*	*SE_M*	*Mean*	*SD*	*SE_M*		
Theoretical	45.00	5.939	.412	42.83	4.716	.394	3.657	S
Economic	44.38	6.110	.424	42.90	6.080	.508	2.224	S
Social	38.03	5.766	.400	39.48	6.074	.508	2.271	S
Political	39.76	5.074	.352	40.33	4.927	.412	1.036	NS
Aesthetic	37.62	6.178	.428	38.31	5.317	.445	1.076	NS
Religious	35.22	7.551	.524	35.99	6.110	.511	1.006	NS

Note: S=Significant at .05 level; NS=Not Significant at .05 level.

The result presented in Table 4.8 indicates the existence of significant difference between undergraduate students of technical and non-technical professional courses with respect to three value dimensions viz theoretical, economic and social. As seen from the analysis that the calculated 't' value of 3.657 for the mean score of technical and non-technical professional course students is significant at .01 level so far theoretical value is concerned. Similarly, with regard to economic and social value the 't' value of 2.224 and 2.271 respectively are also found significant at .05 level.

On the other hand, the calculated 't' value for the mean scores of political, aesthetic and religious value dimensions between technical and non-technical professional course students are found 1.036, 1.076 and 1.006 respectively, which are lower than the critical value of 1.96 at five per cent level of significance. Thus, the Ho_1 stating ***"there is no significant difference between undergraduate students of technical and non-technical professional courses in their value dimensions"*** is partly retained and partly rejected. It is rejected with regard to theoretical, economic and social value dimensions, whereas the hypothesis is retained so far political, aesthetic and religious value dimensions are concerned.

So far theoretical and economic value is concerned, Table 4.8 shows that the students of technical professional courses scored significantly higher (mean score of 45.00 and 44.38 respectively) than the students of non-technical professional courses (mean score of 42.90 and 42.83 respectively); while with respect to social value the students of non-technical professional courses has significantly outscored the students of technical professional courses. Scoring higher on theoretical value by technical professional group than the non-technical professional group appears to be the effects of differential background of both the groups in terms of education, curricular programme, methods of teaching, study habit etc. Except business, all other courses categorised as technical professional in the present study belong to science background, whereas except medicine all other courses categorised as non-technical professional course belong to arts background. Being the science background, the students of technical professional courses are conditioned to be logical, empirical, rational and to the point in their response which the non-technical professional group may not. The methods of instruction of the two types of courses are also different. The technical courses mostly employ empirical investigations, laboratory work, demonstration of facts and relationships aiming at developing precise and realistic outlook whereas non-technical professional courses mostly employ lecture, description etc. aiming at developing wholesome idea and concept. Moreover, there is a general perception that technical courses like engineering, technology etc. demand students with high intellect than courses like education, law, music do. Similarly, scoring significantly higher on economic value by students of technical professional courses than the students of non-technical courses is self-explanatory. Technical courses give back much just as these cost much. These type of courses are directly associated with higher profession as well as income. Again, significant high score of students of non-technical professional courses on social value dimension than their technical counterparts also seems to be the consequences of educational impact. The non-technical professional courses like education, law, music etc. are the reservoir of novel teachings related to life and society. The course on education (B.Ed) trains to become good teacher who in turn is expected to keep the light of society and civilisation burning bright. Music itself produces from social and cultural experiences and meant for developing socialistic attitude. Under such circumstances scoring significantly higher in social value by students of non-technical professional courses than their technical counterpart is adequately justifiable.

Though not much research studies are conducted in line of the present study involving a comparison of value dimensions of students pursuing different types of courses, the result of few studies reported so far goes in the line of the present investigation. The present study reveals that undergraduate students of technical and non-technical professional courses are significantly different with respect to theoretical, economic and social value dimensions. Earlier, Manav, Ram Niwas (1981), Kaur, Amarpreet (1993), Dhekwar, T.M. (1996), and Verma, D. (1996) came out with similar type of results. Manav, Ram Niwas (1981) reported that medical and engineering students differ significantly in social value dimension. According to Kaur, Amarpreet (1993), science male post-graduate students were significantly higher in theoretical and economic value than their arts counterparts. Dhekwar, T.M. (1996) revealed significant difference in theoretical and social value dimensions between higher secondary students of technical/vocational and non-technical courses. Similarly, Verma, D. (1996)

showed that arts college students were higher in social value whereas theoretical value is higher among science and commerce students.

The 't' test has also been employed to determine the significance of difference in the mean scores of value dimensions between male and female undergraduate students of professional courses, which is presented in Table 4.9. The five per cent level of confidence interval is considered to test the significance of 't'.

Table 4.9: Significance of Difference between Mean Scores of Male and Female Undergraduate Students of Professional courses in each of the Six Value Dimensions

Value Dimensions	*Male Students of Professional Courses (N=202)*			*Female Students of Professional Courses (N=149)*			*t-value*	*Status*
	Mean	*SD*	SE_M	*Mean*	*SD*	SE_M		
Theoretical	44.21	5.845	.411	43.98	5.192	.425	.387	NS
Economic	44.57	6.063	.427	42.69	6.077	.498	2.873	S
Social	38.07	6.304	.444	39.37	5.306	.435	2.039	S
Political	41.06	4.817	.339	38.54	4.929	.404	4.798	S
Aesthetic	36.61	5.739	.404	39.65	5.541	.454	4.973	S
Religious	35.46	7.334	.516	35.64	6.546	.536	.241	NS

Note: S=Significant at .05 level; NS=Not Significant at .05 level.

Table 4.9 shows that there is significant difference between male and female undergraduate students of professional courses with respect to four value dimensions namely economic, social, political and aesthetic. The calculated 't' values of 2.873, 2.039, 4.798, 4.973 respectively for the mean scores of economic, social, political and aesthetic value dimensions between male and female students of professional courses has been found significant at 0.05 level, of which the 't' value for two value dimensions (political and aesthetic) are significant even in .01 level. On the other hand, the 't' value of .387 and .241 respectively for theoretical and religious value dimensions are found not significant at 0.05 level.

Male group is significantly higher in economic and political value dimensions (mean scores of 44.57 and 41.06 respectively) than their female counterparts (mean scores of 42.69 and 38.54 respectively).

On the contrary, the female students scored significantly higher in social and aesthetic value dimensions (mean score of 39.37 and 39.65 respectively) than the male students (mean score of 38.07 and 36.61 respectively).

The finding of t-analysis presented in Table 4.9 as males are significantly more economic and political than females, and the females are significantly more social and aesthetic than the males implies that the males are more interested in wealth, luxury as well as in power and influence than females, while females are more interested in relationship, belongingness as well as in form and harmony in comparison to male do. Females as evident find more interest in the artistic episodes of life and try to enjoy each single impression for its own sake in comparison to male, which are generally corroborated to our general observation. Male students are more economic and political, perhaps because of the stereotype of man leading and man dominated system and higher expectations of society and family. Similarly, female students are more social and aesthetic as evident is perhaps owing to the cultural stereotype of being graceful, loving, kind and emotional. Thus, the findings regarding the nature of value dimensions among male and female undergraduate students of professional courses can be amply justified as quite valid and reliable.

The results of most of the previous studies reported so far do support either strongly or partially the results of the present investigation which reveal that male and female undergraduate students of professional courses are significantly different in four value dimensions namely economic, social, political and aesthetic, where male group has significantly outscored the female group with regard to economic and political value whereas the female group has significantly outscored male group in social and aesthetic value. In this line the works of Sati, B. D. (1991) Bauni, Kuotsu (1992) Pradhan, G.C. (1992) Kaur, Amarjeet (1993) Singh, Iqbal (1993) Ranu, Sarbjit Kaur (1995), Singh, R. P. (1997), Bhagawati, Binita (1999), Ghali, Vijayalakshmi (2006), Ferran Casas, Cristina Figuer, Mònica González and Sara Malo (2007), Tripathi, Sujit Ram (2008) etc. are worth mentioning. Resembling the present finding, Sati, B. D. (1991), Bauni, Kuotsu, (1992), Pradhan, G.C. (1992), Ranu, Sarbjit Kaur (1995), Singh, R. P. (1997), Ferran Casas, Cristina Figuer, Mònica González and Sara Malo (2007), and

Tripathi, Sujit Ram (2008), all had concluded that females were higher in social value than their male counterparts. Again, with regard to aesthetic value, Bauni, Kuotsu (1992), Singh, Iqbal (1993), Ranu, Sarbjit Kaur (1995), and Singh, R. P. (1997) have reported in line of the present study that females were significantly higher in aesthetic value than their male counterparts. Again, the findings reported by Kaur, Amarjeet (1993), Singh, Iqbal (1993), Singh, R. P. (1997) and Ferran Casas, Cristina Figuer, Mònica González and Sara Malo (2007) supports the present findings with regard to the difference in economic and political value dimensions between male and female group. Kaur, Amarjeet in 1993 was of the finding that boys of govt. schools were significantly higher in economic value than girl counterparts. Singh, Iqbal (1993) showed significant sex difference in political and economic values. According to Singh, R. P. (1997) male adolescents were significantly higher in the mean scores of economic value than the female adolescent, just as Ferran Casas, Cristina Figuer, Mònica González and Sara Malo (2007) concluded that boys were significantly higher on the materialistic value and the capacities and knowledge related values.

The significance of difference in the mean scores of different value dimensions between male and female undergraduate students of technical and non-technical professional courses are also calculated separately. The result of 't' analysis in value dimensions of male and female students of technical professional courses is presented in Table 4.10. The five per cent level of confidence interval is considered to test the significance of 't'.

Table 4.10 shows that there is significant difference between male and female undergraduate students of technical professional courses with respect to two value dimensions namely political and aesthetic. The calculated 't' value of 2.716 and 2.310 respectively for political and aesthetic value dimensions are found significant at .05 level of confidence interval. On the other the calculated 't' value of .009, 1.184, .966 and .185 respectively for theoretical, economic, social and religious value dimensions are found lower than the critical value even at .05 level, hence not insignificant. Of the significant differences in two value dimensions, the male group is found higher in political value with mean scores of 40.43 than their female counterparts with mean scores of

Table 4.10: Significance of Difference between Mean Scores of Male and Female Undergraduate Students of Technical Professional courses in each of the Six Value Dimensions

Value Dimensions	*Male Students of Technical Professional Courses (N=138)*			*Female Students of Technical Professional Courses (N=70)*			*t-value*	*Status*
	Mean	*SD*	*SE_M*	*Mean*	*SD*	*SE_M*		
Theoretical	45.03	6.104	.520	44.94	5.644	.675	.099	NS
Economic	44.73	6.056	.516	43.67	6.197	.741	1.184	NS
Social	37.75	5.826	.496	38.57	5.648	.675	.966	NS
Political	40.43	4.845	.412	38.44	5.288	.632	2.716	S
Aesthetic	36.93	6.077	.517	39.00	6.188	.740	2.310	S
Religious	35.15	7.873	.670	35.36	6.926	.828	.185	NS

Note: S=Significant at .05 level; NS=Not Significant at .05 level.

38.44. On the contrary, the female students are found significantly higher in aesthetic value with mean score of 39.00 than the male students with mean score of 36.93.

The 't' analysis in mean scores of different value dimensions between male and female students of non-technical professional courses is also made and presented in Table 4.11. The five per cent level of confidence interval is considered to test the significance of 't'.

Table 4.11: Significance of Difference between Mean Scores of Male and Female Undergraduate Students of Non-Technical Professional courses in each of the Six Value Dimensions

Value Dimensions	*Male Students of Non-Technical Professional Courses (N=64)*			*Female Students of Non-Technical Professional Courses (N=79)*			*t-value*	*Status*
	Mean	*SD*	*SE_M*	*Mean*	*SD*	*SE_M*		
Theoretical	42.45	4.837	.605	43.13	4.625	.520	.848	NS
Economic	44.23	6.112	.764	41.82	5.872	.661	2.398	S
Social	38.75	7.233	.904	40.08	4.911	.553	1.301	NS
Political	42.42	4.500	.562	38.63	4.619	.520	4.934	S
Aesthetic	35.94	4.908	.614	40.23	4.865	.547	5.223	S
Religious	36.11	6.014	.752	35.89	6.224	.700	.217	NS

Note: S=Significant at .05 level; NS=Not Significant at .05 level.

Male and female undergraduate students of non-technical professional courses are significantly different in the mean scores of three value dimensions namely, economic, political and aesthetic as evident in the result presented in Table 4.11. The calculated 't' value for the mean scores of economic, political and aesthetic values between the two groups are found as 2.398, 4.934 and 5.223 respectively, which are higher than the critical value of 1.96 at .05 level, hence significant. On the other hand, the calculated 't' value of .848, 1.301 and .217 for theoretical, social and religious value dimensions respectively between male and female students of non-technical professional courses are lower than the critical value at .05 level of significance. Hence, there is no significant difference between male and female students of non-technical professional with regard to theoretical, social and religious value dimensions. Of the significant mean differences in three value dimensions, the male group is found significantly higher in economic and political value and the female group is found significantly higher in aesthetic value than their counterparts.

It is here to be noted that the t-analysis of value dimensions between male and female undergraduates of non-technical professional courses shows similar type of results as held between male and female undergraduates of technical professional courses as well as male and female students of professional courses as a whole. In all cases, male group is found significantly higher in political value and significantly lower in aesthetic value than their female counterparts. Thus, it may be inferred that a change in type of courses may not significantly influence in weightage of mean scores of value dimensions among male and female students at undergraduate level.

The significance of difference in the mean scores of different value dimensions between male undergraduate students of technical and non-technical professional courses as well as female undergraduate students of technical and non-technical professional courses are also calculate separately. The results of 't' analysis in value dimensions of male students of technical and non-technical professional courses is presented in Table 4.12. The five per cent level of confidence interval is considered to test the significance of 't'.

Table 4.12: Significance of Difference between Mean Scores of Male Undergraduate Students of Technical and Non-technical Professional courses in each of the Six Value Dimensions

Value Dimensions	*Male Students of Technical Professional Courses (N=138)*			*Male Students of Non-Technical Professional Courses (N=64)*			*t-value*	*Status*
	Mean	*SD*	*SE_M*	*Mean*	*SD*	*SE_M*		
Theoretical	45.03	6.104	.520	42.45	4.837	.605	2.970	S
Economic	44.73	6.056	.516	44.23	6.112	.764	.542	NS
Social	37.75	5.826	.496	38.75	7.233	.904	1.045	NS
Political	40.43	4.845	.412	42.42	4.500	.562	2.773	S
Aesthetic	36.93	6.077	.517	35.94	4.908	.614	1.142	NS
Religious	35.15	7.873	.670	36.11	6.014	.752	-.863	NS

Note: S=Significant at .05 level; NS=Not Significant at .05 level.

Table 4.12 shows that there is significant difference between male undergraduate students of technical and non-technical professional courses with respect to two value dimensions namely, theoretical and political. The calculated 't' value of 2.970 and 2.773 respectively for theoretical and political value dimensions are found significant at 0.05 level. On the other hand, the calculated 't' value for the remaining four value dimensions i.e. economic, social, aesthetic and religious are found as .542, 1.045, 1.142 and .863 respectively, which are lower than the critical value of 1.96 at five per cent level of confidence interval. Thus, the differences between the two groups with regard to economic, social, aesthetic and religious value dimensions are statistically insignificant.

Out of the significant differences in two value dimensions, the male students of technical professional courses are found significantly higher in theoretical value dimension than male students of non-technical professional courses, while the later group is found significantly higher in political value dimension than the former group.

The 't' analysis in the mean scores of different value dimensions between female undergraduate students of technical and non-technical professional courses is also made and presented in Table 4.13. The five per cent level of confidence interval is considered to test the significance of 't'.

Table 4.13: Significance of Difference between Mean Scores of Female Undergraduate Students of Technical and Non-technical Professional courses in each of the Six Value Dimensions

Value Dimensions	*Female Students of Technical Professional Courses (N=70)*			*Female Students of Non-Technical Professional Courses (N=79)*			*t-value*	*Status*
	Mean	*SD*	SE_M	*Mean*	*SD*	SE_M		
Theoretical	44.94	5.644	.675	43.13	4.625	.520	2.157	S
Economic	43.67	6.197	.741	41.82	5.872	.661	1.869	NS
Social	38.57	5.648	.675	40.08	4.911	.553	1.739	NS
Political	38.44	5.288	.632	38.63	4.619	.520	.234	NS
Aesthetic	39.00	6.188	.740	40.23	4.865	.547	1.354	NS
Religious	35.36	6.926	.828	35.89	6.224	.700	.491	NS

Note: S=Significant at .05 level; NS=Not Significant at .05 level.

As seen from the analysis in Table 4.13 that the ‘t’ value of 2.157 for the mean score of theoretical value dimension between female students of technical and non-technical professional course is significant at .05 level of significance. The ‘t’ value of remaining five value dimensions namely, economic, social, political, aesthetic and religious are found as 1.869, 1.739, .234, 1.354 and .491 respectively, which are lower than the critical value of 1.96 at .05 level. Thus, there is significant difference between female undergraduate students of technical and non-technical professional courses in theoretical value dimension, where the former group has scored significantly higher with mean scores of 44.94 than the later group with mean scores of 43.13. The difference between the two groups with regard to economic, social, political, aesthetic and religious value dimensions are found statistically insignificant, though remarkable difference is observed between the two groups with respect to economic, social and aesthetic value dimensions, where the females of technical courses scored relatively higher in economic value, while the females of non-technical professional courses scored remarkably higher in social and aesthetic value dimensions.

Objective-3: *To study the level of aspiration of undergraduate students of both technical and non-technical professional courses of Gauhati University.*

Ho$_2$: *There is no significant difference between undergraduate students of technical and non-technical professional courses in their level of aspiration score.*

In order to answer the third objective, analysis has been made by calculating the mean scores and standard deviations of level of aspiration separately for the students of technical and non-technical professional courses. To test the hypothesis, 't' test has been employed on the mean scores of level of aspiration between the two groups. Moreover, three criterion groups as High Aspirant Group, Moderate Aspirant Group and Low Aspirant Group are identified for both technical and non-technical professional course students separately on the basis of highest 33 per cent, middle 34 per cent and lowest 33 per cent score of level of aspiration of the respective target group, as per the suggestions of the author of the *Level of Aspiration Measure (LOA)*. Thereafter, total counts as well as percentage of cases falling in each of the three criterion groups are calculated.

Table 4.14: Mean scores and 't' value of Undergraduate Students of Technical and Non-Technical Professional Courses in Level of Aspiration, and Percentages of students under different aspiration level of both the groups

Category	*Level of Aspiration*											
	Mean	*SD*	*SE_M*	*'t' value*	*Status*	*Range*	*High Aspirant*		*Moderate Aspirant*		*Low Aspirant*	
							No.	*%*	*No.*	*%*	*No.*	*%*
Students of Technical Professional Courses (N=208)	3.33	1.89	.131	3.90	S	7.0	60	28.9	80	38.5	68	32.7
Students of Non-Technical Professional Courses (N=143)	2.61	1.42	.119			5.8	34	23.8	61	42.7	48	33.6

Note: S indicates significant at .05 level of confidence interval.

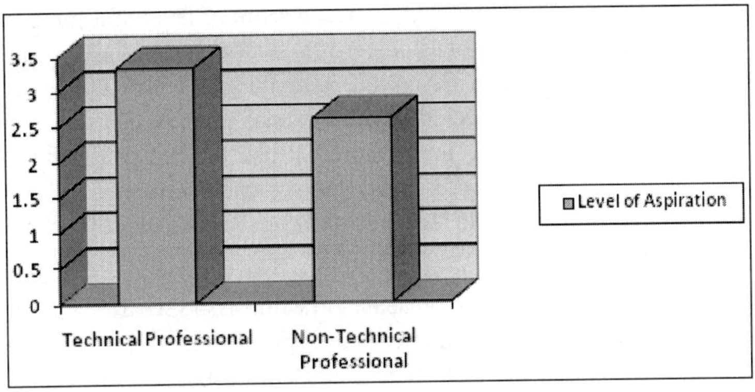

Figure 9: Graphical Representation of Mean scores of Level of Aspiration of Undergraduate Students of Technical and Non-Technical Professional Courses.

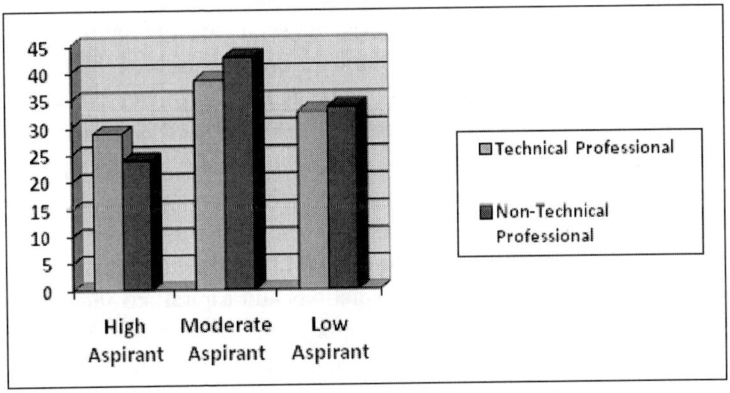

Figure 10: Graphical Representation of percentage of High, Moderate and Low Aspirant Undergraduate Students of Technical and Non-Technical Professional Courses.

The mean scores, the 't' value on level of aspiration score of technical and non-technical professional course students, and also the number and percentage of students with different levels of aspiration for both the groups are calculated and presented in Table 4.14. The mean scores of level of aspiration of technical and non-technical professional course students are graphically represented through Figure 9. Figure 10 represents the percentage of High Aspirant, Moderate Aspirant and Low Aspirant students of both technical and non-technical professional courses.

The Table 4.14 reveals that the mean score of level of aspiration of undergraduate students of technical professional courses is 3.33 with S.D. of 1.89, whereas the mean score is found 2.61 with S.D. of 1.42 for the students of non-technical professional courses. Thus, on the basis of weightage of the mean scores, it can be said that students belonging to technical professional courses endorse higher level of aspiration in comparison to the students of non-technical professional courses do.

The result of the 't-test' presented in Table 4.14 reveals that there is significant difference in the level of aspiration score between the undergraduate students of technical and non-technical professional courses. The calculated 't' value of level of aspiration score of students of technical vs non-technical professional courses is found 3.90 which is greater than the critical value of 2.58 at .01 level of confidence interval. Hence, difference does exist between the two groups in their level of aspiration score where the later group outscored the former group. As such the Ho_2 stating ***"there is no significant difference between undergraduate students of technical and non-technical professional courses in their level of aspiration score"*** is fully rejected. This finding is corroborated with the finding reported by Harbison (1991) who in his study to investigate the career aspirations of the students pursuing MSW degree revealed that those holding the BSW degree have different career expectations and aspirations than those who do not hold this degree. The implication of the present finding is that nature of education being exposed is one of the significant factors influencing the goal setting behaviour of undergraduate students. The difference as evident may be attributed to the impact of differential educational experiences of both the groups. The technical courses are generally associated with higher level of expectations, opportunities, job positions etc. A bright and very specific vision remains clear in front of the students pursuing these types of courses which may not in case of the students of non-technical professional courses. Moreover, the parental as well as social expectations from the students of technical courses remain relatively higher. All these factors perhaps contribute to set their future goal to a higher level.

The table further reveals that 60, 80 and 68 number of cases out of a total of 208 is high, moderate and low aspirant respectively for the students of technical professional courses which accounted at 28.9 per cent, 38.5 per cent and 32.7 per cent respectively. On the other hand, 34, 61 and 48 number of cases out of a total of 143 is high, moderate and low aspirant respectively in case of students of non-technical professional courses which translated into 23.8 per cent, 42.7 per cent and 33.6 per cent respectively. Thus, it is observed that the percentage of high aspirant is higher among students of technical professional courses than the students of non-technical professional courses, whereas the percentage of moderate and low aspirant is higher in the later group than the former group.

Table 4.15: Mean scores and 't' value of Male and Female Undergraduate Students of Professional Courses in Level of Aspiration, and Percentages of students under different aspiration level of both the groups.

Category	*Level of Aspiration*											
	Mean	*SD*	*SE_M*	*'t' value*	*Status*	*Range*	*High Aspirant*		*Moderate Aspirant*		*Low Aspirant*	
							No.	*%*	*No.*	*%*	*No.*	*%*
Male Students of Professional Courses (N=202)	3.11	1.79	.126	.958	NS	7.1	44	21.8	81	40.1	77	38.1
Female Students of Professional Courses (N=149)	2.93	1.69	.138			6.9	28	18.8	64	43	57	38.3

Note: NS indicates not significant at .05 level of confidence interval.

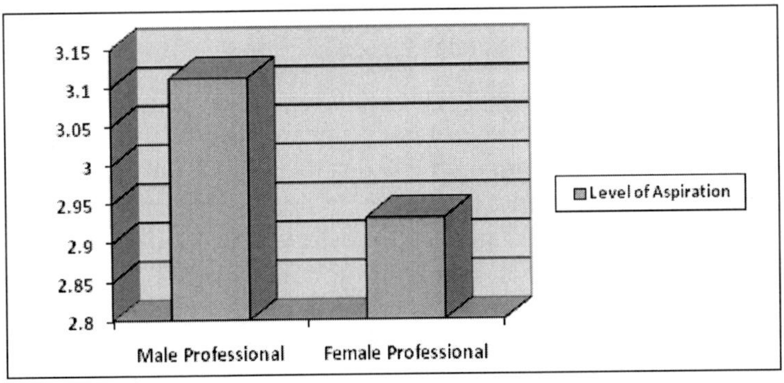

Figure 11: Graphical Representation of Mean scores of Level of Aspiration of Male and Female Undergraduate Students of Professional Courses.

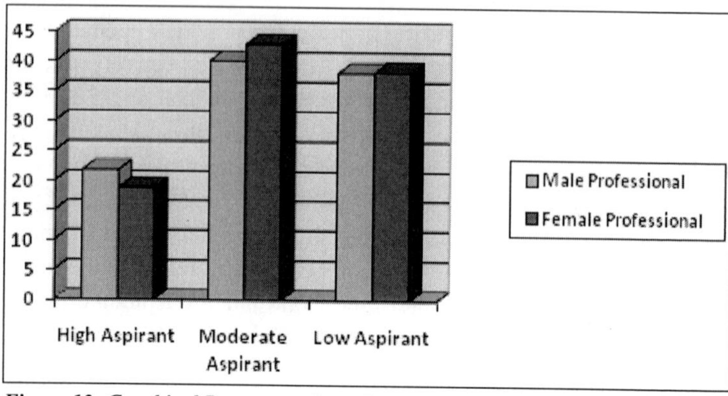

Figure 12: Graphical Representation of percentage of High, Moderate and Low Aspirant Male and Female Undergraduate Students of Professional Courses.

The investigator has also tried to investigate the gender difference on level of aspiration of undergraduate students of professional courses. The mean scores and 't' value of level of aspiration score of male and female undergraduate students of professional course is calculated and presented in Table 4.15. Moreover, the percentages of High, Moderate and Low aspirant students for both the groups are calculated on the basis of highest 33 per cent, middle 34 per cent and lowest 33 per cent score of level of aspiration of the respective target group, as per the suggestion of the author of the Level of Aspiration Measure (LOA), which is also presented in Table 4.15. The mean score of level of aspiration of male and female students of professional courses is graphically presented in Figure 11. Again, the percentages of high, moderate and low aspirant male and female students of professional courses are represented through Figure 12.

The Table 4.15 shows that the mean score of level of aspiration of male undergraduate students of professional courses is 3.11 with S.D. of 1.79, whereas the mean score is found 2.93 with S.D. of 1.69 for their female counterparts. Thus, on the basis of weightage of the mean scores, it is observed that male undergraduate students of professional courses endorse higher aspiration in comparison to the female undergraduate students of professional courses. This finding is corroborated with our general observation with people in male dominated Indian culture and also supported by the findings reported by Kruezer (1992) and Wilgenbusch and Merrell (1999). Kruezer (1999) in his study on 311 university seniors reported that female have lower aspiration to leader and hopeless in their career than do men. According to Wilgenbusch and Merrell (1999), in spite of having equivalent talent or test scores to males, the girls were found to endorse lower levels of self-confidence in their abilities and in their mathematical aspirations.

The result of the 't-test' presented in table 4.15 reveals that there is no significant difference in level of aspiration score between male and female undergraduate students of professional courses. The calculated 't' value of level of aspiration of male vs female students of professional courses is found .958, which is lower than the critical value of 1.96 at .05 level. Thus, male group though remarkably higher in level of aspiration score than the female group, yet the difference is not so high to make it statistically significant. This finding goes in line with the findings reported by Bhatt, P. D. (2005), who in a comparative study with regard to level of aspiration, revealed that sex had no role in creating educational as well as personal aspiration among sports person. Another contradictory finding was reported by Pathak, M. (2002), who showed that male undergraduates were significantly higher on educational aspiration than their female counterparts. The contradiction between the finding of the present study and that of Pathak, M. (2002) is perhaps because of the variances in the target population, sample size, tools and techniques between the two studies. Pathak, M. (2002) conducted his study on undergraduate students of all types of courses, where as the present study covers only the undergraduate students of professional courses. Being the students of professional courses, the females are expected to set their future goal to a higher level than the females in general.

The Table 4.15 also shows that 44, 81 and 77 number of students out of a total of 202 is high, moderate and low aspirants respectively in case of male group which accounted at 21.8 per cent, 40.1 per cent and 38.1 per cent respectively. On the other hand, 28, 64 and 57 number of students out of a total of 149 is found high, moderate and low aspirant respectively so far the female undergraduate students of professional courses are concerned which translated in to 18.8 per cent, 43 per cent and 38.3 per cent respectively. Thus, it is observed that the percentage of high aspirant is higher among the male students of professional courses than their female counterparts, whereas the percentage of moderate aspirant is higher in the female group than their male counterparts. In case of low aspirant, the percentage is found almost similar between the two groups of samples.

The investigator has calculated the mean scores and 't' value of level of aspiration score of male and female undergraduate students of technical professional courses and also calculated the percentages of high, moderate and low aspirants among the two groups on the basis of highest 33 per cent, middle 34 per cent and lowest 33 per cent score of level of aspiration of the respective group, as per the suggestion of the author of the Level of Aspiration Measure (LOA), which are presented in Table 4.16. The result is also graphically represented through Figure 13 and Figure 14.

Table 4.16: Mean scores and 't' value of Male and Female Undergraduate Students of Technical Professional Courses in Level of Aspiration, and Percentages of students under different aspiration level of both the groups

Category	*Level of Aspiration*											
	Mean	*SD*	SE_M	*'t' value*	*Stat-us*	*Range*	*High Aspirant*		*Moderate Aspirant*		*Low Aspirant*	
							No.	*%*	*No.*	*%*	*No.*	*%*
Male Students of Technical Professional Courses (N=138)	3.42	1.93	.164	.967	NS	7.0	42	30.4	52	37.7	44	31.9
Female Students of Technical Professional Courses (N=70)	3.15	1.81	.217			6.8	21	30	28	40	21	30

Note: NS indicates not significant at .05 level of confidence interval.

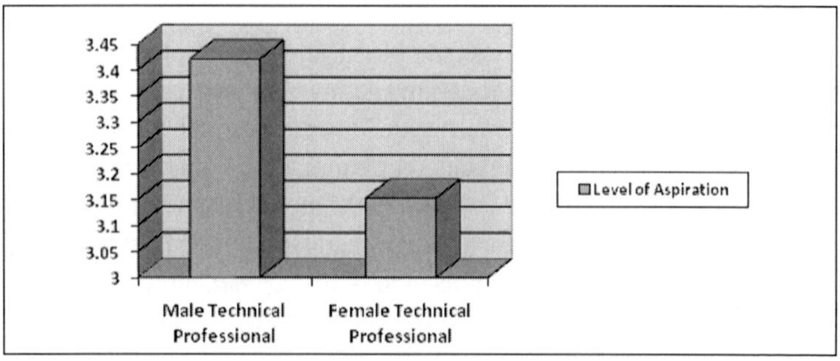

Figure 13: Graphical Representation of Mean scores of Level of Aspiration of Male and Female Undergraduate Students of Technical Professional Courses.

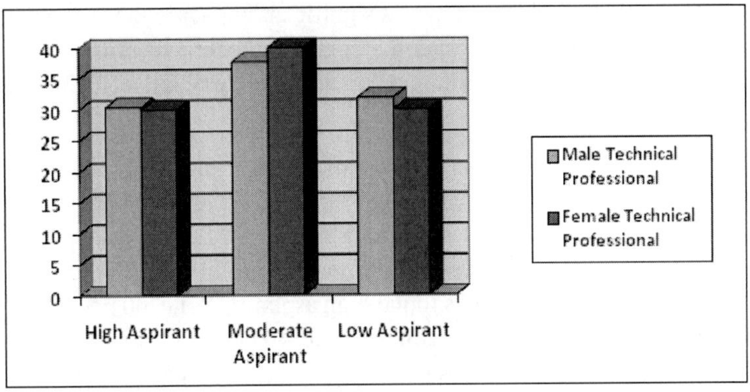

Figure 14: Graphical Representation of percentage of High, Moderate and Low Aspirant Male and Female Undergraduate Students of Technical Professional Courses.

The mean score of level of aspiration of male undergraduate students of technical professional courses is 3.42 with S.D. of 1.93, whereas the mean score is found 3.15 with S.D. of 1.81 for their female counterparts as evident in Table 4.16. Thus, on the basis of weightage of mean scores of both the groups, it can be said that male undergraduate students of technical professional courses endorse higher level of aspiration in comparison to the female group do. It is here to be mentioned that male students of professional courses as a whole are also found relatively higher in level of aspiration score than their female counterpart. Thus, it can be inferred that the nature of goal setting behaviour of both male as well as female undergraduate students of technical professional courses are similar to that of the students of professional courses as a whole.

The result of the 't-test' presented in Table 4.16 reveals that though male students of technical professional courses scored slightly higher than their female counterparts in level of aspiration, the difference is not statistically significant even at 05 level. The calculated 't' value of the mean score of level of aspiration between male and female students of technical professional courses is found .967 which is lower than the critical value at .05 level. Hence, the difference is not statistically significant. This finding also goes in line of the result evident for the male and female students of professional courses as a whole. Thus, it is inferred that sex does not have a significant impact in the change of level of aspiration score among students of technical professional courses which also follows the finding reported by Bhatt, P. D. (2005).

So far the number of students with different levels of aspiration is concerned, Table 4.16 depicts that out of a total of 138 samples of male students 42 i.e. 30.43 per cent is high aspirant, 52 i.e. 37.68 per cent is moderate aspirant and the remaining 44 i.e. 31.88 per cent is low aspirant. Similarly, with regard the female group out of a total of 70 cases 21 i.e. 30 per cent is found high aspirant, 28 i.e. 40 per cent is moderate aspirant and the remaining 21 i.e. 30 per cent is low aspirant. Thus, no remarkable divergence is observed between the male and female undergraduate students of technical professional courses so far the percentage of cases with different level of aspiration is concerned.

Similar to the male and female of technical professional courses, the investigator has also calculated the mean scores and 't' value of level of aspiration score of male and female undergraduate students of non-technical professional courses and also calculated the percentages of high, moderate and low aspirants among the two groups on the basis of highest 33 per cent, middle 34 per cent and lowest 33 per cent score of level of aspiration

Table 17: Mean scores and 't' value of Male and Female Undergraduate Students of Non-Technical Professional Courses in Level of Aspiration, and Percentages of students under different aspiration level of both the groups.

Category	*Level of Aspiration*											
	Mean	*SD*	*SE$_M$*	*'t' value*	*Status*	*Range*	*High Aspirant*		*Moderate Aspirant*		*Low Aspirant*	
							No.	*%*	*No.*	*%*	*No.*	*%*
Male Students of Non-Technical Professional Courses (N=64)	2.45	1.24	.155	1.21	NS	5.1	15	23.4	31	48.4	18	28.1
Female Students of Non-Technical Professional Courses (N=79)	2.73	1.55	.175			5.8	22	27.9	32	40.5	25	31.7

Note: NS indicates not significant at .05 level of confidence interval.

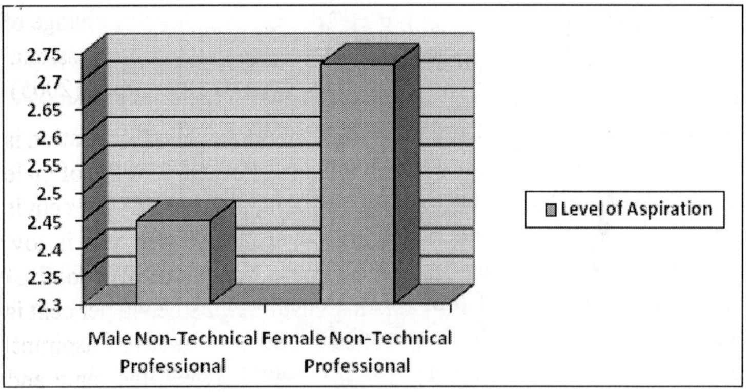

Figure 15: Graphical Representation of Mean scores of Level of Aspiration of Male and Female Undergraduate Students of Non-Technical Professional Courses.

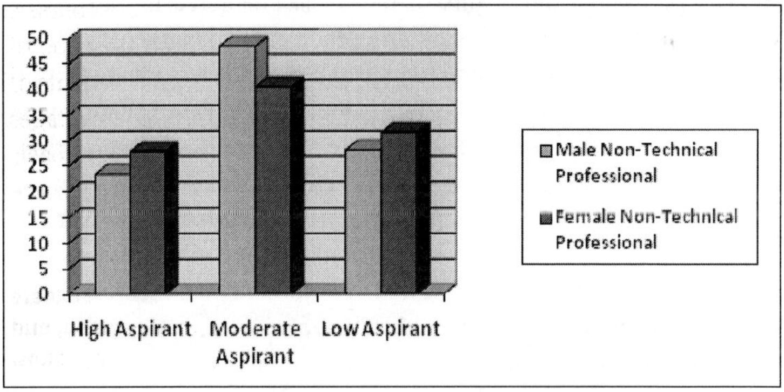

Figure 16: Graphical Representation of percentage of High, Moderate and Low Aspirant Male and Female Undergraduate Students of Non-Technical Professional Courses.

of the respective group, as per the suggestion of the author of the Level of Aspiration Measure (LOA), which are presented in Table 4.17. The mean score of level of aspiration of male and female students of non-technical professional courses and the percentages of high, moderate and low aspirant male and female students of non-technical professional courses are graphically represented through Figure 15 and Figure 16 respectively.

The result presented in Table 4.17 shows that the mean score of level of aspiration of male undergraduate students of non-technical professional courses is 2.45 with S.D. of 1.24, whereas it is 2.73 with S.D. of 1.55 for their female counterparts. Thus, with the help of mean scores of both the groups, it is perceived that female undergraduate students of non-technical professional courses are slightly higher in level of aspiration score in comparison to the male group. Thus, a contradictory finding is reported with regard to level of aspiration score of male and female students of non-technical professional courses. In earlier cases i.e. males and females of technical professional courses; and male and females of professional courses as a whole, the male group outscored the female group. But in case of non-technical professional courses the female group is found higher than the male group. Thus, it can be said that nature of course influences the goal setting behaviour of both the sexes of professional education.

The perusal of the results of the 't-test' depicted in Table 4.17 reveals that there is no significant difference in the mean score of level of aspiration between male and female undergraduate students of non-technical professional courses. The calculated 't' value of the mean score of level of aspiration between male and female students of non-technical professional courses is found 1.21 which is lower than the critical value at .05 level. Hence, the difference is not statistically significant, though it is observed that female group with a mean score of 2.73 has slightly outscored the male group with mean score of 2.45. It is here to be mentioned that the difference between male and female undergraduate students in their level of aspiration in all types of courses under consideration i.e. technical professional courses, non-technical professional courses and professional courses as a whole, is found statistically insignificant at .05 level. Hence, it can be strongly argued that irrespective of nature or type of education, sex does not contribute significantly in causing a difference in level of aspiration score among the undergraduate students of professional courses. Hence, the findings reported by Bhatt, P. D. (2005), who stated that sex had no role in creating educational as well as personal aspiration among sports person, closely fits with the present observations and findings.

So far the number of students with different levels of aspiration is concerned, Table 4.17 reveals that out of a total of 64 samples of male students 15, 31 and 18 are high, moderate and low aspirant respectively which accounted at 23.4 per cent, 48.4 per cent and 28.1 per cent respectively. Similarly, in case of female group out of a total of 79 cases, 22 i.e. 27.9 per cent is high aspirant, 32 i.e. 40.5 per cent is moderate aspirant and the remaining 25 i.e. 31.7 per cent is low aspirant. Thus, the percentage of high and low aspirant is higher among the female group in comparison to male group, whereas the percentage of moderate aspirant student is higher among the later group than the former group.

As significant difference does exist in level of aspiration score between undergraduate students of technical and non-technical professional courses, therefore the researcher has intended to find out where actually the difference lies? Whether it is in between male students of technical and non-technical professional courses or in-between female students of technical and non-technical professional courses, or among both the gender? The researcher, therefore, has calculated the mean scores and 't' value of level of aspiration between male students of technical and non-technical professional courses, and also identified the percentages of high, moderate and low aspirants among the two groups on the basis of highest 33 per cent, middle 34 per cent and lowest 33 per cent score of level of aspiration of the respective group, as per the suggestion of the author of the Level of Aspiration Measure (LOA), which are presented in Table 4.18. The result is graphically represented through Figure 17 and Figure 18.

Table 4.18 : Mean scores and 't' value of Male Undergraduate Students of Technical and Non-Technical Professional Courses in Level of Aspiration, and Percentages of students under different aspiration level of both the groups.

Category	*Level of Aspiration*											
	Mean	*SD*	*SE_M*	*'t' value*	*Status*	*Range*	*High Aspirant*		*Moderate Aspirant*		*Low Aspirant*	
							No.	*%*	*No.*	*%*	*No.*	*%*
Male Students of Technical Professional Courses (N=138)	3.42	1.93	.164	3.71	S	7.0	42	30.4	52	37.7	44	31.9
Male Students of Non-Technical Professional Courses (N=64)	2.45	1.24	.155			5.1	15	23.4	31	48.4	18	28.1

Note: S indicates significant at .05 level of confidence interval.

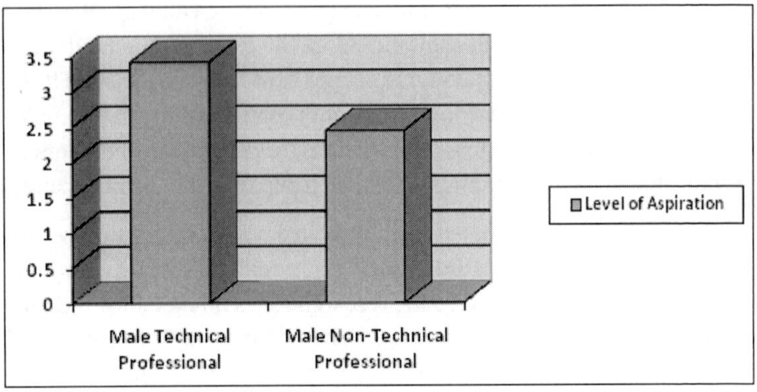

Figure 17: Graphical Representation of Mean scores of Level of Aspiration of Male Undergraduate Students of Technical and Non-Technical Professional Courses.

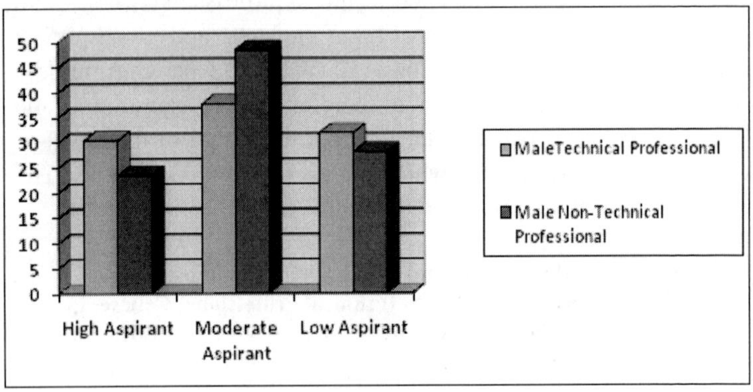

Figure 18: Graphical Representation of percentage of High, Moderate and Low Aspirant Male Undergraduate Students of Technical and Non-Technical Professional Courses.

The result presented in Table 4.18 reveals that the mean score of level of aspiration of male undergraduate students of technical professional courses is 3.42 with S.D. of 1.93. On the other hand the mean score for male students of non-technical professional courses is found 2.45 with S.D. of 1.24. Thus, remarkable variance is observed in the mean scores of level of aspiration between the male undergraduate students of technical and non-technical professional courses. The result of the 't-test' reveals that the calculated 't' value of the mean scores of level of aspiration of male undergraduate students of technical vs non-technical professional courses is 3.71 which is greater than the critical value of 2.58 at .01 level. Hence, difference does exist between the two groups in their level of aspiration, where the males of technical courses significantly outscored the males of non-technical professional courses. It is here to be mentioned that irrespective of sex, the undergraduate students of technical professional courses as a whole also scored significantly higher than the students of non-technical professional courses as evident in Table 4.14. This finding is also held for the present case i.e. in case of male students of technical and non-technical professional courses.

The Table 4.18 also shows that 42, 52 and 44 number of students out of a total of 138 endorse high, moderate and low level of aspiration respectively in case of male students of technical professional courses which accounted at 30.4 per cent, 37.7 per cent and 31.9 per cent respectively. On the other hand, 15, 31 and 18 number of students out of a total of 64 is found to endorse high, moderate and low level of aspiration respectively so far the male undergraduate students of non-technical professional courses are concerned, which translated in to 23.4 per cent, 48.4 per cent and 28.1 per cent respectively. Thus, it is observed that the percentage of high as well as low aspirant is higher among the male students of technical professional courses than the males of non-technical professional courses, where as the percentage of moderate aspirant is higher among the later group than the former group. The researcher, has calculated the mean scores and 't' value of level of aspiration score between female undergraduate students of technical and non-technical professional courses, and also identified the percentage of high, moderate and low aspirants among the two groups on the basis of highest 33 per cent, middle 34 per cent and lowest 33 per cent score of level of aspiration of the respective group, as per the suggestion of the author of the Level of Aspiration Measure (LOA), which are presented in Table 4.19. The result is graphically represented through Figure 19 and Figure 20.

Table 4.19: Mean scores and 't' value of Female Undergraduate Students of Technical and Non-Technical Professional Courses in Level of Aspiration, and Percentages of students under different aspiration level of both the groups

Category	*Level of Aspiration*											
	Mean	*SD*	*SE$_M$*	*'t' value*	*Status*	*Range*	*High Aspirant*		*Moderate Aspirant*		*Low Aspirant*	
							No.	*%*	*No.*	*%*	*No.*	*%*
Female Students of Technical Professional Courses (N=70)	3.15	1.81	.217	1.52	NS	6.8	21	30	28	40	21	30
Female Students of Non-technical Professional Courses (N=79)	2.73	1.55	.175			5.8	22	27.9	32	40.5	25	31.7

Note: NS indicates not significant at .05 level of confidence interval.

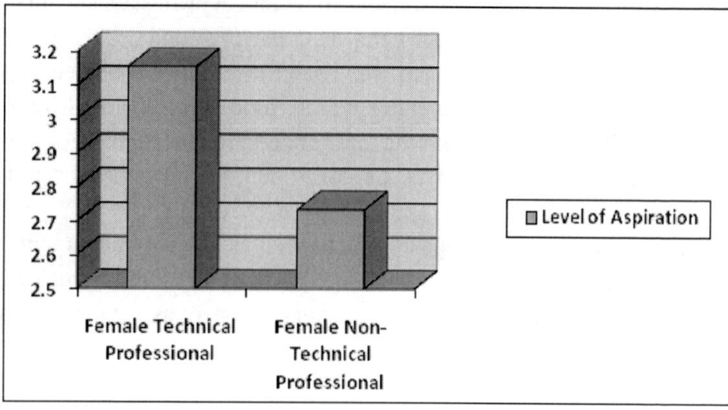

Figure 19: Graphical Representation of Mean scores of Level of Aspiration of Female Undergraduate Students of Technical and Non-Technical Professional Courses.

The Table 4.19 reveals that the mean score of level of aspiration of female undergraduate students of technical professional courses is 3.15 with S.D. of 1.81, while the mean score is found 2.73 with S.D. of 1.55 for female students of non-technical professional courses. Thus, notable difference is observed in the mean scores of level of aspiration between the female undergraduate students of technical and non-technical professional courses, where the females of technical

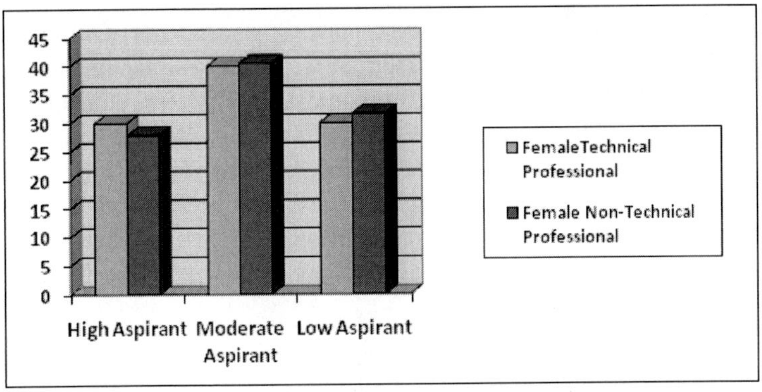

Figure 20: Graphical Representation of percentage of High, Moderate and Low Aspirant Female Undergraduate Students of Technical and Non-Technical Professional Courses.

professional courses scored higher than the females of non-technical professional courses. However, the result of the 't-test' shows that the difference is not statistically significant at .05 level. The calculated 't' value of the mean scores of level of aspiration of female undergraduate students of technical vs non-technical professional courses is found 1.52 which is lower than the critical value of 1.96 at .05 level.

It is to be noted that the difference in the mean scores of level of aspiration is found significant between the students of technical and non-technical professional courses as a whole as evident in Table 4.14, and between the male undergraduate students of technical and non-technical professional courses as evident in Table 4.18. Here, in case of female students of technical and non-technical professional courses, though the difference is not statistically significant yet found quiet remarkable with t-value of 1.52. Hence, it can be concluded that irrespective of their sex, nature of education influences the level of aspiration score of undergraduate students of professional courses, significantly in case of male students and considerably in case of female students.

Further, Table 4.19 shows that 21, 28 and 21 number of students out of a total of 70 is high, moderate and low aspirant respectively in case of female students of technical professional courses which accounted at 30 per cent, 40 per cent and 30 per cent respectively.

On the other hand, 22, 32 and 25 number of students out of a total of 79 is high, moderate and low aspirant respectively so far the female undergraduate students of non-technical professional courses are concerned, which translated in to 27.9 per cent, 40.5 per cent and 31.7 per cent respectively. Thus, the percentage of high aspirant is higher among the female students of technical professional courses than the females of non-technical professional courses, where as the percentage of moderate and low aspirant is higher among the later group than the former group.

The mean scores of level of aspiration and also the percentage of students with high, moderate and low level of aspiration has been calculated for the undergraduate students of professional courses as a whole, which are presented in Table 4.20. The percentages of high, moderate and low aspirant students of professional courses are also graphically represented through Figure 21.

Table 4.20: Mean scores and SD of Level of Aspiration of Undergraduate Students of Professional Courses, and Percentages of students under different aspiration level

Category	*Level of Aspiration*								
	Mean	*SD*	*Range*	*High Aspirant*		*Moderate Aspirant*		*Low Aspirant*	
				No.	*%*	*No.*	*%*	*No.*	*%*
Undergraduate Students of Professional Courses (N=351)	3.04	1.75	7.1	72	20.5	145	41.3	134	38.2

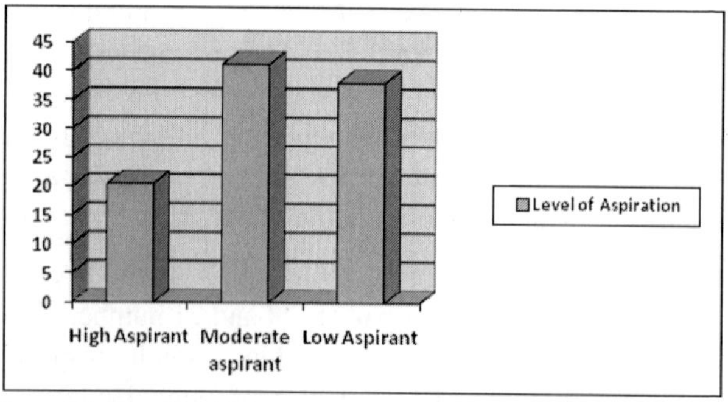

Figure 21: Graphical Representation of percentage of Undergraduate Students of Professional Courses with different Levels of Aspiration.

Table 4.20 reveals that the mean score of level of aspiration of undergraduate students of professional courses is 3.15 with S.D. of 1.75. It is also observed that out of a total of 351 samples 72 i.e. 20.5 per cent of students of professional courses are high aspirant, 145 i.e. 41.3 per cent students are moderate aspirant, whereas the remaining 134 cases i.e. 38.2 per cent students belongs to low level of aspiration.

Thus, the detailed analysis from Table 4.14 to 4.20 concentrates on the mean scores and 't' value of level of aspiration score as well as the percentage of cases with high, moderate and low level of aspiration of the samples constituted sex-wise and nature of course-wise. The results reveal that the mean score of level of aspiration of undergraduate students of technical professional courses is higher than the students of non-technical professional courses. It is also observed that the percentage of high aspirant student is higher among the students of technical professional courses than their non-technical counterparts. Sex-wise analysis of technical and non-technical professional courses also depicts similar results. Both male and female of technical professional courses tend to higher in the mean scores on their level of aspiration than their non-technical professional counterparts. Thus, it is perceived that irrespective of their gender the students of technical professional courses are higher in comparison to the students of non-professional courses are higher in comparison to the students of non-technical professional courses so far their goal setting behaviour is concerned.

Exploring the factors of level of aspiration though not under the purview of the present study, yet the higher level of aspiration among students of technical professional courses than their non-technical professional counterparts as evident can be attributed to the impact of education. **Bond, R., and Saunders, P. (1999)**, in their study showed that children's aspirations were positively related to their test scores. This implies that aspirations is influenced and raised by their ability. Children's abilities and talents play an important role in the development of their aspirations. As it is an accepted fact that only the students with high abilities and talents in terms of their achievement goes and can succeed in technical courses which are mainly rooted in science background, the result of the present investigation as students of technical professional courses endorse higher aspiration than the students of non-technical professional courses closely fits with that of the results reported by **Bond, R., and Saunders, P. (1999).**

Again, sex-wise analysis reveals that male undergraduate students of professional courses tend to endorse higher level of aspiration in comparison to the female students of professional courses. Similarly, the percentage of high aspirant is found higher among male than female undergraduates of professional courses. These findings go in the line of the findings of Kruezer (1992) and Wilgenbusch and Merrell (1999). Kruezer (1992) in his study on 311 university seniors reported that females have lower aspiration to leader and hope less in their career than do men. According to Wilgenbusch and Merrell (1999), in spite of having equivalent talent or test scores to males, the girls were found to endorse lower levels of self-confidence in their abilities and in their mathematical aspirations.

Lower aspiration among females than males may be attributed to the impact of different factors like gender role stereotypes, perceptions of sexism, self-confidence, perception or self-concept of their abilities etc. Females are most of the times treated as granted and not given the due respect and importance in different socio-economic endeavours even in modern Indian society. An attitude of inferiority used to grow among females from the early years of their life. Such cultural stereotype and attitude of being subordination might be one of the causes of low aspiration among females in India which is also reported by the present study.

Objective-4: *To determine the relationship between value dimensions and level of aspiration of undergraduate students of technical and non-technical professional courses.*

Ho_3 : *There is no significant relationship between value dimensions and level of aspiration of undergraduate students of technical and non-technical professional courses.*

In order to answer the fourth objective, Pearson's Correlation test has been employed. The coefficients of correlation of each of the six value dimensions with level of aspiration score are calculated separately for students of technical and non-technical professional courses, which are presented in Table 4.21. To test the significance of 'r', .05 level of confidence interval is taken into consideration in all cases.

Table 4.21: Coefficients of Correlation between scores on Level of Aspiration and each of the Six Value Dimensions of Undergraduate Students of Technical and Non-Technical Professional courses.

Variables		*Students of Technical Professional Courses (N=208)*				*Students of Non-Technical Professional Courses (N=143)*			
		M	*SD*	*r*	*Status*	*M*	*SD*	*r*	*Status*
Value Dimensions	Theoretical	45.00	5.94	.203	S	42.83	4.72	.162	NS
	Economic	44.38	6.11	.086	NS	42.90	6.08	.273	S
	Social	38.03	5.77	.020	NS	39.48	6.07	-.075	NS
	Political	39.76	5.07	-.043	NS	40.33	4.93	-.105	NS
	Aesthetic	37.62	6.18	-.060	NS	38.31	5.32	-.062	NS
	Religious	35.22	7.55	-.164	S	35.99	6.11	.199	S
Level of Aspiration		3.33	1.89	----	----	2.61	1.42	----	----

Note: S= Significant at .05 level; NS= Not Significant at .05 level.

The above Table 4.21 depicting the relationship of scores on level of aspiration score and value dimensions separately for undergraduate students of technical and non-technical professional courses reveals that level of aspiration is positively correlated with three value dimensions namely, theoretical, economic and social with 'r' value of .203, .087, and .020 respectively, and negatively correlated with political, aesthetic and religious value dimensions with 'r' value of -.043, -.060 and -.164 respectively so far the undergraduate students of technical professional courses are concerned. Thus, from the 'r' values it is observed that the correlations of level of aspiration with most of the value dimensions are slight and almost negligible. However, in general it can be inferred that higher the level of aspiration score the more they are the rational, practical, economic, social and helpful in nature in their day-do-day dealings. On the other hand, increase in level of aspiration accompanies a decrease in political, aesthetic and religious values of students of technical professional courses as evident.

Similarly, with regard to the students of non-technical professional courses, it is found that level of aspiration is positively correlated with theoretical and economic value dimensions with 'r' value of .162 and .273 respectively, while negatively correlated with social, political, aesthetic and religious value dimensions with 'r' value of -.075, -.105, -.062 and -.199 respectively. Thus, the relationship of level of aspiration score with economic and religious value dimensions are low, while with regard to the remaining four value dimensions the correlations are slight and almost negligible. Thus, variance is observed between students of technical and non-technical professional courses with regard to the nature of relationship of level of aspiration and social value dimension. It is found positive in case of the former group while negative in case of the later group.

So far the status of statistical significance is concerned, Table 4.21 further reveals that there is significant correlation between scores on level of aspiration and two value dimensions namely theoretical and religious in case of the students of technical professional courses. The relationship of level of aspiration score with remaining four value dimensions namely economic, social, political and aesthetic are statistically not significant. As such, Ho_3 stating ***'there is no significant relationship between value dimensions and level of aspiration of undergraduate students of technical and non-technical professional courses'*** is rejected with regard to theoretical and religious value dimensions so far undergraduate students of technical professional courses are concerned. But the hypothesis is retained for the same group with regard to economic, social, political and aesthetic value dimensions.

Again, with regard to the relationship of scores on level of aspiration with value dimensions of undergraduate students of non-technical professional courses, it is found that level of aspiration score is significantly correlated with two value dimensions namely, economic and religious. The coefficients of correlation of level of aspiration with remaining four value dimensions namely, theoretical, social, political and aesthetic has not reached the level of statistical significance at .05 levels. Thus, the Ho_3 stating ***'there is no significant relationship between value dimensions and level of aspiration of undergraduate***

students of technical and non-technical professional courses' is rejected with regard to economic and religious value dimensions so far students of non-technical professional courses are concerned. But the hypothesis is retained for the students of same group with regard to theoretical, social, political and aesthetic value dimensions. Thus, it is observed that religious value dimension is significantly correlated with level of aspiration score in case of undergraduate students of both technical and non-technical professional courses. In both cases the correlation is negative, implying that irrespective of nature of course, higher the level of aspiration score the lower the score on religious value among undergraduate students of professional courses or vice-versa.

Objective-5: *To determine the relationship between value dimensions and level of aspiration of male and female undergraduate students of professional courses.*

Ho_4 : *There is no significant relationship between value dimensions and level of aspiration of male and female undergraduate students of professional courses.*

Table 4.22: Coefficients of Correlation between scores on Level of Aspiration and each of the Six Value Dimensions of Male and Female Undergraduate Students of Professional courses

Variables		*Male Students of Professional Courses (N=202)*				*Female Students of Professional Courses (N=149)*			
		M	*SD*	*r*	*Status*	*M*	*SD*	*r*	*Status*
Value Dimensions	Theoretical	44.21	5.85	.188	S	43.98	5.19	.227	S
	Economic	44.57	6.06	.156	S	42.69	6.08	.171	S
	Social	38.07	6.30	-.006	NS	39.37	5.31	-.077	NS
	Political	41.06	4.82	-.116	NS	38.54	4.93	-.050	NS
	Aesthetic	36.61	5.74	-.009	NS	39.65	5.54	-.135	NS
	Religious	35.46	7.33	-.183	S	35.64	6.55	-.176	S
Level of Aspiration		3.11	1.79	----	----	2.93	1.69	----	----

Note: S= Significant at .05 level; NS= Not Significant at .05 level.

In order to answer the fifth objective, Pearson's Correlation test has been employed. The coefficients of correlation of each of the six value dimensions with level of aspiration score are calculated separately for male and female undergraduate students of professional courses, which are presented in Table 4.22. To test the significance of 'r', .05 level of confidence interval is taken into consideration.

The result of the relationship of scores on level of aspiration and each of the six value dimensions shows almost similar findings for male and female undergraduate students of professional courses as depicted in Table 4.22. It is observed that level of aspiration score is positively correlated with two value dimensions in case of both male and female undergraduate students of professional courses. These are theoretical and economic with 'r' value of .188 and .156 respectively for the male group and .227 and .171 respectively for the female group. But, out of these positive correlations, only the relationship between scores of level of aspiration and theoretical value dimension of female group is found definite, while the remaining correlations are slight and almost negligible. Thus, it is evident that an increase or decrease in the magnitude of level of aspiration brings corresponding increase or decrease in the scores of theoretical and economic value dimensions for both male and female undergraduate students of professional courses. The higher the level of aspiration score the more they are the rational, practical and economic or vice-versa, in their day-to-day dealings or in financial matters.

On the other hand, level of aspiration score is negatively correlated with the remaining four value dimensions namely social, political, aesthetic and religious in case of both male and female undergraduate students of professional courses with 'r' value of -.006, -.116, -.009 and -.183 respectively for male group and -.077, -.050, -.135 and -.176 respectively for the female group. But, all these relationships are very slight and almost negligible as evident. Still, it may be said that higher the level of aspiration score the lower the scores on social, political, aesthetic and religious value dimensions of both male and female undergraduate students of professional courses.

So far the significance of 'r' is concerned, Table 4.22 reveals that level of aspiration score is significantly correlated at .05 level with three value dimensions for both the groups. These are theoretical, economic and religious. The relationship of level of aspiration score with remaining three value dimensions namely, social, political and aesthetic are not statistically significant at .05 level in case of both male and female students. As such, Ho_4 stating ***'there is no significant relationship between value dimensions and level of aspiration of male and female undergraduate students of professional courses'*** is rejected for three value dimensions and accepted for three value dimensions for both the groups. It is rejected with regard to theoretical, economic and religious value dimensions, while retained with regard to social, political and aesthetic value dimensions for both male and female undergraduate students of professional courses. This result goes in line of the result documented by Ranu, Sarbjit Kaur (1995), who showed that theoretical value was significantly correlated with level of aspiration of both male and female post-graduate students. It is here to be noted that the relationship of level of aspiration score with theoretical and economic value dimensions are found significantly positive, whereas the relationship of level of aspiration score with religious value dimension is found significantly negative for both male and female students.

Thus, complete identity is recorded for the result of coefficients of correlation of level of aspiration score and each of the six value dimensions between male and female undergraduate students of professional courses. The inference of the finding is that gender may not interfere in the relationship between level of aspiration score and value dimensions so far the undergraduate students of professional courses are concerned.

As significant relationship does exist between scores on level of aspiration with theoretical and religious value dimensions in case of students of technical professional courses as a whole as evident in Table 4.21, therefore the investigator has tried to investigate whether there is any significant relationship between the two variables in case of male and female students of these courses. The results of Pearson's Coefficients of Correlation between scores on level of aspiration and each of the six value dimensions are presented separately for male and female students of technical professional courses in Table 4.23.

Table 4.23: Coefficients of Correlation between scores on Level of Aspiration and each of the Six Value Dimensions of Male and Female Undergraduate Students of Technical Professional Courses

Variables		*Male Students of Technical Professional Courses (N=138)*				*Female Students of Technical Professional Courses (N=70)*			
		M	*SD*	*r*	*Status*	*M*	*SD*	*r*	*Status*
Value Dimensions	Theoretical	45.03	6.10	.172	S	44.94	5.64	.274	S
	Economic	44.73	6.06	.092	NS	43.67	6.20	.057	NS
	Social	37.75	5.83	.032	NS	38.57	5.65	.008	NS
	Political	40.43	4.85	-.089	NS	38.44	5.29	.006	NS
	Aesthetic	36.93	6.08	-.028	NS	39.00	6.19	-.095	NS
	Religious	35.15	7.87	-.149	NS	35.36	6.93	-.198	NS
Level of Aspiration		3.421	1.93	----	----	3.153	1.81	----	----

Note: S= Significant at .05 level; NS= Not Significant at .05 level.

The above Table 4.23 reveals that level of aspiration score is positively correlated with three value dimensions namely, theoretical, economic and social with 'r' value of .172, .092, and .032 respectively, while negatively correlated with political, aesthetic and religious value dimensions with 'r' value of -.089, -.028 and -.149 respectively so far the male undergraduate students of technical professional courses are concerned. Thus, it is evident that the relationship between scores on level of aspiration and all the value dimensions of male group are slight and almost negligible. Again, with regard to the female students of technical professional courses the level of aspiration score is found positively correlated with four value dimensions namely, theoretical, economic, social and political with 'r' value of .274, .057, .008 and .006 respectively, while negatively correlated with aesthetic and religious value dimensions with 'r' value of -.095 and -.198 respectively. But among these, only the relationship with regard to theoretical value dimension is found definite, while with regard to remaining value dimensions the relationships are slight and almost negligible. It needs to be focused that variance is observed between male and female students of technical professional courses with regard to the relationship of scores on level of aspiration and political value dimension. It is found negative in case of the former group while positive in case of the later group.

So far the status of statistical significance is concerned, Table 4.23 reveals that level of aspiration is significantly correlated with theoretical value for both the groups. No other value dimension out of economic, social, political, aesthetic and religious is significantly correlated with level of aspiration score in case of both male and female group, though in case of religious value dimension the magnitude of relationship is found relatively higher for both the groups. These are -.149 and .198 respectively for male and female group.

It is to be noted that the result of the relationship of scores on level of aspiration and value dimensions of male students of technical professional courses remains same as that recorded for the students of technical professional courses as a whole irrespective of their gender. Level of aspiration score is positively correlated with theoretical, economic and social value dimensions and negatively correlated with political, aesthetic and social value dimensions for students of technical professional courses as a whole which remains intact for the male group of that courses as evident. Variance is observed with respect to female group. Four value dimensions namely, theoretical, economic, social and political are positively correlated with level of aspiration score in case of female group of technical professional courses, whereas in case of the total group irrespective of their sex, theoretical, economic and social value dimensions are positively correlated with level of aspiration score. That means, political value is positively correlated with level of aspiration score of female students of technical professional courses, where as it is negatively correlated in case of the students of technical professional courses as a whole.

The investigator has tried to investigate the relationship of the scores on level of aspiration with different value dimensions separately for male and female undergraduate students of non-technical professional courses through employing Pearson's Coefficients of Correlation technique, which are presented in Table 4.24.

Table 4.24: Coefficients of Correlation between scores on Level of Aspiration and each of the Six Value Dimensions of Male and Female Undergraduate Students of Non-Technical Professional Courses

Variables		*Male Students of Non-Technical Professional Courses (N=64)*				*Female Students of Non-Technical Professional Courses (N=79)*			
		M	*SD*	*r*	*Status*	*M*	*SD*	*r*	*Status*
Value Dimensions	Theoretical	42.45	4.84	.028	NS	43.13	4.63	.245	S
	Economic	44.23	6.11	.362	S	41.82	5.87	.263	S
	Social	38.75	7.23	-.039	NS	40.08	4.91	-.142	NS
	Political	42.42	4.50	-.009	NS	38.63	4.62	-.111	NS
	Aesthetic	35.94	4.91	-.041	NS	40.23	4.87	-.161	NS
	Religious	36.11	6.01	-.288	S	35.89	6.22	-.143	NS
Level of Aspiration		2.445	1.24	----	----	2.734	1.55	----	----

Note: S= Significant at .05 level; NS= Not Significant at .05 level

The result of the relationship as presented in Table 4.24 reveals almost similar observations for male and female undergraduate students of non-technical professional courses. It is found that level of aspiration score is positively correlated with two value dimensions in case of both male and female undergraduate students of non-technical professional courses. These are theoretical and economic with 'r' value of .028 and .362 respectively for the male group and .245 and .263 respectively for the female group. Thus, it can be inferred that, an increase or decrease in the magnitude of level of aspiration score brings corresponding increase or decrease in the scores of theoretical and economic value dimensions for both male and female undergraduate students of non-technical professional courses. On the other hand, level of aspiration is negatively correlated with the remaining four value dimensions namely, social, political, aesthetic and religious in case of both male and female undergraduate students of non-technical professional courses with 'r' value of -.039, -.009, -.041 and -.288 respectively for male group and -.142, -.111, -.161 and -.143 respectively for the female group. Among these correlations in both the group, the correlation between level of aspiration score and religious value dimension of male group is found definite and the remaining relationships are slight and almost negligible. However, in general it can be said that higher the level of aspiration score, the lower the scores on these four value dimensions of both male and female undergraduate students of non-technical professional courses.

The Table 4.24 further reveals that level of aspiration score is significantly correlated with economic (positive) and religious (negative) value dimensions of male students of non-technical professional courses at .05 level of confidence interval. The relationship of scores on level of aspiration and remaining four value dimensions namely, theoretical, social, political and aesthetic values of male group are found much nominal and hence their influence upon each other is negligible. On the other hand, with regard to the female group, it is observed that level of aspiration score is significantly correlated with theoretical and economic value dimensions, while it is not significantly correlated with remaining four value dimensions namely, social, political, aesthetic and religious.

It is here to be noted that the result of the relationship of scores on level of aspiration and value dimensions of both male and female students of non-technical professional courses remains same as that recorded for the students of non-technical professional courses as a whole irrespective of their gender. In all the three cases i.e. total group, male group and female group, level of aspiration is positively correlated with theoretical and economic value dimensions whereas negatively correlated with social, political, aesthetic and religious value dimensions. Thus, it can be inferred that gender does not influence in the relationship of scores on level of aspiration and each of the six value dimensions so far the students of non-technical professional courses are concerned.

The result of the relationship of scores on level of aspiration and different value dimensions of male students of technical and non-technical professional courses are also presented together in Table 4.25, in order to have an understanding of the nature of relationship between the two variables in case of male group of different types of courses.

Table 4.25: Coefficients of Correlation between scores on Level of Aspiration and each of the Six Value Dimensions of Male Undergraduate Students of Technical and Non-Technical Professional courses

Variables		*Male Students of Technical Professional Courses (N=138)*				*Male Students of Non-Technical Professional Courses (N=64)*			
		M	*SD*	*r*	*Status*	*M*	*SD*	*r*	*Status*
Value Dimensions	Theoretical	45.03	6.10	.172	S	42.45	4.84	.028	NS
	Economic	44.73	6.06	.092	NS	44.23	6.11	.362	S
	Social	37.75	5.83	.032	NS	38.75	7.23	-.039	NS
	Political	40.43	4.85	-.089	NS	42.42	4.50	-.009	NS
	Aesthetic	36.93	6.08	-.028	NS	35.94	4.91	-.041	NS
	Religious	35.15	7.87	-.149	NS	36.11	6.01	-.288	S
Level of Aspiration		3.421	1.93	----	----	2.445	1.24	----	----

Note: S= Significant at .05 level; NS= Not Significant at .05 level.

The Table 4.25 reveals that level of aspiration score is positively correlated with three value dimensions namely, theoretical, economic and social with ‘r’ value of .172, .092, and .032 respectively, while negatively correlated with political, aesthetic and religious value dimensions with ‘r’ value of -.089, -.028 and -.149 respectively so far the male undergraduate students of technical professional courses are concerned. Thus, the correlations of level of aspiration score with all the value dimensions are slight and almost negligible for male group of technical professional courses. On the other hand, level of aspiration score is positively correlated with two value dimensions in case of male undergraduate students of non-technical professional courses. These are theoretical and economic with ‘r’ value of .028 and .362 respectively, while negatively correlated with social, political, aesthetic and religious value dimensions with ‘r’ of -.039, -.009, -.041 and -.288. Thus, it is seen that the relationship of level of aspiration score with regard to economic and religious values are definite, while with regard to remaining four values the relationships are slight and almost negligible so far the male students of non-technical professional courses are concerned.

The Table 4.25 further reveals that level of aspiration score is significantly correlated with only one value dimension in case of male students of technical professional courses i.e. theoretical value with 'r' value of .172, while it is significantly correlated with economic (positive) and religious (negative) value dimensions of male students of non-technical professional courses with 'r' value of .362 and -.288 respectively. The relationship of level of aspiration with remaining five value dimensions of male technical professional group namely, economic, social, political, aesthetic and religious and remaining four value dimensions of male non-technical professional group namely, theoretical, social, political and aesthetic are very nominal and statistically insignificant.

Similar to the male group of technical and non-technical professional courses, the researcher has also presented the results of 'r' test between the scores on level of aspiration and different value dimensions of female group of technical and non-technical professional courses in Table 4.26.

Table 4.26: Coefficients of Correlation between scores on Level of Aspiration and each of the Six Value Dimensions of Female Undergraduate Students of Technical and Non-Technical Professional courses

Variables		*Female Students of Technical Professional Courses (N=70)*				*Female Students of Non-Technical Professional Courses (N=79)*			
		M	*SD*	*r*	*Status*	*M*	*SD*	*r*	*Status*
Value Dimensions	Theoretical	44.94	5.64	.274	S	43.13	4.63	.245	S
	Economic	43.67	6.20	.057	NS	41.82	5.87	.263	S
	Social	38.57	5.65	.008	NS	40.08	4.91	-.142	NS
	Political	38.44	5.29	.006	NS	38.63	4.62	-.111	NS
	Aesthetic	39.00	6.19	-.095	NS	40.23	4.87	-.161	NS
	Religious	35.36	6.93	-.198	NS	35.89	6.22	-.143	NS
Level of Aspiration		3.153	1.81	----	----	2.734	1.55	----	----

Note: S= Significant at .05 level; NS= Not Significant at .05 level.

The result presented in Table 4.26 reveals that level of aspiration score is positively correlated with four value dimensions namely, theoretical, economic, social and political with 'r' value of .274, .057,

.008 and .006 respectively, while negatively correlated with aesthetic and religious value dimensions with 'r' value of -.095, and -.198 respectively so far the female undergraduate students of technical professional courses are concerned. Thus, low correlation is observed between scores on level of aspiration and theoretical value, whereas the relationships of level of aspiration with remaining five value dimensions are slight and almost negligible so far the female group of technical professional courses are concerned. On the other hand, level of aspiration score is positively correlated with two value dimensions namely theoretical and economic with 'r' value of .245 and .263 respectively; and negatively correlated with social, political, aesthetic and religious value dimensions with 'r' value of -.142, -.111, -.161, -.143 respectively in case of female students of non-technical professional courses. Here also, the correlations of level of aspiration score with theoretical and economic values are low, while with regard to remaining four values the correlations are slight and almost negligible.

The Table 4.26 further reveals that level of aspiration score is significantly correlated with only one value dimension in case of female students of technical professional courses i.e. theoretical value with 'r' value of .274, while level of aspiration score is significantly correlated with economic and religious value dimensions of female students of non-technical professional courses with 'r' value of .245 and .263 respectively. The relationship of level of aspiration score with remaining five value dimensions of female technical professional group namely, economic, social, political, aesthetic and religious and remaining four value dimensions of female non-technical professional group namely, social, political, aesthetic and religious are very nominal and statistically insignificant.

Thus, finally it can be inferred that an increase or decrease in the score on level of aspiration corresponds a significant increase or decrease in score of theoretical value dimension or vice-versa among female undergraduate students of technical professional courses. On the contrary, with regard to female students of non-technical professional courses, an increase or decrease in the score of level of aspiration corresponds a significant increase or decrease in scores of theoretical and economic value dimensions or vice-versa.

The researcher has also intended to investigate the relationship between scores on level of aspiration and different value dimensions of undergraduate students of professional courses as a whole, which are presented in Table 4.27.

Table 4.27: Coefficients of Correlation between scores on Level of Aspiration and each of the Six Value Dimensions of Undergraduate Students of Professional courses

Variables		*Undergraduate Students of Professional Courses (N=351)*			
		M	*SD*	*r*	*Status*
Value Dimensions	Theoretical	44.11	5.57	.223	S
	Economic	43.77	6.13	.168	S
	Social	38.62	5.93	-.038	NS
	Political	39.99	5.02	-.073	NS
	Aesthetic	37.90	5.84	-.071	NS
	Religious	35.53	7.00	-.181	S
Level of Aspiration		3.035	1.75	-----	-----

Note: S= Significant at .05 level; NS= Not Significant at .05 level.

Table 4.27 depicting the result of correlations between value dimensions and level of aspiration score of undergraduate students of professional courses reveals that level of aspiration score is positively correlated with theoretical and economic value dimensions with 'r' value of .223 and .168 respectively, while negatively correlated with remaining four value dimensions namely, social, political, aesthetic and religious 'r' value of -.038, -.073, -.071 and -.181 respectively. Thus, low correlation is observed between scores on level of aspiration and theoretical value dimension, whereas the correlation of level of aspiration score with remaining five value dimensions are slight and almost negligible.

So far the level of statistical significance is concerned, the table further reveals that level of aspiration score is significantly correlated with three value dimensions. These are theoretical, economic and religious with 'r' value of .223, .168 and -.181 respectively.

The relationship of level of aspiration score with remaining three value dimensions namely, social, political and aesthetic has not reached the level of statistical significance at .05 level.

The foregoing analysis concentrates on examining the coefficients of correlations between scores on level of aspiration and different value dimensions of the sample constituted sex-wise and nature of course-wise. The result reveals that theoretical, economic and religious value dimensions are significantly correlated with level of aspiration score among most of the groups of samples. The remaining three value dimensions namely, social, political and aesthetic are not significantly correlated with level of aspiration score in any of the target group.

So far the students of technical and non-technical professional courses are concerned, it is observed that level of aspiration score is significantly correlated with theoretical and religious value dimensions in case of technical professional group, while with theoretical and economic value dimensions in case of non-technical professional group. Thus, variance is observed between the two groups in the relationship of level of aspiration score with two value dimensions (economic and religious). In case of students of technical professional courses level of aspiration is significantly correlated with religious value but not with economic value, which is reverse in case of the students of non-technical professional courses.

Sex-wise analysis of correlation reveals complete identity among male and female students of professional courses. It is found that level of aspiration score is significantly correlated with theoretical, economic and religious value dimensions among both male and female undergraduate students of professional courses. The remaining three value dimensions namely social, political and aesthetic are not significantly correlated with score on level of aspiration of both male and female students. This result goes in line of the result documented by Ranu, Sarbjit Kaur (1995), who showed that theoretical value is significantly correlated with level of aspiration of both male and female post-graduate students.

With regard to the male and female students of technical and non-technical professional courses, it is observed that level of aspiration score is significantly correlated with only theoretical value dimension of both male and female group of technical professional courses. The relationships with remaining five value dimensions are statistically insignificant for both the groups. On the other hand, level of aspiration score is significantly correlated with economic and religious value dimensions of male group, and with theoretical and economic value dimensions of female group so far the non-technical professional courses are concerned. Theoretical, social, political and aesthetic value dimensions of male group and social, political, aesthetic and religious value dimension of female group of non-technical professional courses are not significantly correlated with level of aspiration score.

Thus, in the pertinent, it is perceived that level of aspiration score is not significantly correlated with social, political and aesthetic value dimensions in any of the target group whether it is technical and non-technical professional group, male and female professional group, male and female of technical professional group or male and female of non-technical professional group. Hence, it can be rightly inferred that nature of courses and gender may not influence significantly in the nature of relationship of level of aspiration score with social, political and aesthetic value dimensions.

Objective-6: *To examine whether there is significant difference in the relationship of value dimensions and level of aspiration between undergraduate students of technical and non-technical professional courses.*

Ho_5 : *There is no significant difference in the relationship of value dimensions and level of aspiration between undergraduate students of technical and non-technical professional courses.*

The 'r' value of each of the six value dimensions with level of aspiration score for both the groups i.e. students of technical and non-technical professional courses are converted into 'z' scores and then the standard error of the difference between the 'z' scores of the two groups are calculated. Afterwards, significance of difference between two 'r' (Z's) is determined through using the following formula, the result of which is presented in Table 4.28. To test the significance of difference between two 'r' (Z's), .05 level of confidence interval is taken into consideration in all cases.

$$CR = \frac{Z_1 - Z_2}{SE_{Diff}(Z)}$$

Table 4.28: Significance of Difference in the Relationship of scores on Level of Aspiration and each of the Six Value Dimensions between Undergraduate Students of Technical and Non-Technical Professional Courses

Value Dimensions	*Students of Technical Professional Courses (N=208)*		*Students of Non-Technical Professional Courses (N=143)*		*SE Diff (Z)*	*CR*	*Status*
	r-value	*z-value*	*r-value*	*z-value*			
Theoretical	.20	.20	.16	.16	.11	.36	NS
Economic	.09	.09	.27	.28	.11	1.73	NS
Social	.02	.02	-.08	-.08	.11	.91	NS
Political	-.04	-.04	-.11	-.11	.11	.64	NS
Aesthetic	-.06	-.69	-.06	-.06	.11	00	NS
Religious	-.16	-.16	-.20	-.20	.11	.36	NS

Note: S= Significant at .05 level; NS= Not Significant at .05 level.

As seen from the Table 4.28 that the 'CR' of .36, 1.73, .91, .64, 00, .36 between technical and non-technical professional courses students for the relationship of level of aspiration score and six value dimensions namely, theoretical, economic, social, political, aesthetic and religious respectively are much lower than 1.96 to be significant at .05 level. Hence, significant difference does not exist between the students of technical and non-technical professional courses in the relationship of level of aspiration score and any of the six value dimensions. As such, Ho_5 stating, ***"there is no significant difference in the relationship of value dimensions and level of aspiration between undergraduate students of technical and non-technical professional courses"*** is fully retained. It is accepted for the relationships of level of aspiration score and each of the six value dimensions under consideration.

However, the table shows that the correlation between level of aspiration score and theoretical value dimension of technical professional group is slightly stronger than the non-technical professional group with 'r' value of -.20 and .16 respectively for the two groups, while the relationship of level of aspiration score with four value dimensions of non-technical professional group namely, economic, social, political and religious are slightly stronger than their technical professional counterparts with 'r' value of .27, -.08, -.11 and -.20 respectively for the technical professional group and .09, .02, -.04 and -.16 respectively for non-technical professional group. With regard to aesthetic value dimension both the groups are equal with 'r' value of -.06. Thus, though maximum difference between the two groups is recorded with regard to the relationship of level aspiration score and economic value dimension, yet it is not statistically significant at .05 level of confidence interval. Thus, it may be inferred that level of aspiration exerts more or less similar type of influence upon the six value dimensions among the students of both technical and non-technical professional courses. Change in the type of education may not accompany a significant variance in the nature of relationship between level of aspiration and value dimensions.

Objective-7: *To examine whether there is significant difference in the relationship of value dimensions and level of aspiration between male and female undergraduate students of professional courses.*

Ho_6 : *There is no significant difference in the relationship of value dimensions and level of aspiration between male and female undergraduate students of professional courses.*

In order to answer the seventh objective, the 'r' value of each of the six value dimensions with level of aspiration score for both the groups i.e. male and female undergraduate students of professional courses are converted into 'z' scores and then the standard error of the difference between the 'z' scores of the two groups are calculated. Afterwards, significance of difference between two 'r' (Z's) is determined through using the following formula, the result of which is presented in Table 4.29. To test the significance of difference between two 'r' (Z's), .05 level of confidence interval is taken into consideration in all cases.

$$\mathbf{CR} = \frac{\mathbf{Z_1 - Z_2}}{SE_{Diff}(Z)}$$

Table 4.29: Significance of Difference in the Relationship of scores on Level of Aspiration and each of the Six Value Dimensions between Male and Female Undergraduate Students of Professional Courses

Value Dimensions	*Male Students of Professional Courses (N=202)*		*Female Students of Professional Courses (N=149)*		SE_{Diff} *(Z)*	*CR*	*Status*
	r-value	*z-value*	*r-value*	*z-value*			
Theoretical	.19	.19	.23	.23	.11	.36	NS
Economic	.16	.16	.17	.17	.11	.09	NS
Social	-.01	-.01	-.08	-.08	.11	.64	NS
Political	-.12	-.12	-.05	-.05	.11	.64	NS
Aesthetic	-.01	-.01	-.14	-.14	.11	1.18	NS
Religious	-.18	-.18	-.18	-.18	.11	00	NS

Note: S= Significant at .05 level; NS= Not Significant at .05 level.

From the perusal of the results contained in the Table 4.29 it is clear that there is no significant difference in the relationship of scores of level of aspiration and each of the six value dimensions between male and female undergraduate students of professional courses. The 'CR' value for the relationship of level of aspiration score with theoretical, economic, social, political, aesthetic and religious value dimensions between the two groups are found .36, .09, .64, .64, 1.18 and 0 respectively, which are much lower than 1.96 to be significant at .05 level of confidence interval. Hence, significant difference does not exist between male and female undergraduate students of professional courses in the relationship of level of aspiration score and any of the six value dimensions. As such Ho_6 stating, ***"there is no significant difference in the relationship of value dimensions and level of aspiration between male and female undergraduate students of professional courses"*** is fully retained. It is accepted for the relationships of level of aspiration score with each of the six value dimensions under consideration.

However, the table shows that the correlation between level of aspiration score and political value dimension of male group is slightly stronger than the female group with 'r' value of -.12 and .05 respectively, while the relationship of level of aspiration score with four value dimensions namely, theoretical, economic, social and aesthetic of female group are slightly higher than their male counterparts with 'r' value of .23, .17, -.08 and -.14 respectively for the female group and .19, .16, -.01 and -.01 respectively for male group. With regard to religious value dimension both the groups are equal with 'r' value of -.18. Thus, though maximum difference between male and female group is recorded with regard to the relationship of level aspiration score and aesthetic value dimension, yet it is not statistically significant even at .05 level of confidence interval. Hence, it may be inferred that level of aspiration exerts more or less similar types of influence upon the value dimensions among both male and female undergraduate students of professional courses. Gender may not cause a significant variance in the nature of relationship between level of aspiration and value dimensions as evident.

The researcher has also compared the relationship of scores on level of aspiration and different value dimensions between male and female students of technical professional courses, which are presented in Table 4.30.

Table 4.30: Significance of Difference in the Relationship of scores on Level of Aspiration and each of the Six Value Dimensions between Male and Female Undergraduate Students of Technical Professional Courses

Value Dimensions	*Male Students of Technical Professional Courses (N=138)*		*Female Students of Technical Professional Courses (N=70)*		*SE_{Diff} (Z)*	*CR*	*Status*
	r-value	*z-value*	*r-value*	*z-value*			
Theoretical	.17	.17	.27	.28	.15	.73	NS
Economic	.09	.09	.06	.06	.15	.20	NS
Social	.03	.03	.01	.01	.15	.13	NS
Political	-.09	-.09	.01	.01	.15	.67	NS
Aesthetic	-.03	-.03	-.10	-.10	.15	.47	NS
Religious	-.15	-.15	-.20	-.20	.15	.33	NS

Note: S= Significant at .05 level; NS= Not Significant at .05 level.

The result of significance of difference in the relationship of scores on level of aspiration and each of the six value dimensions between male and female students of technical professional courses as presented in Table 4.30 reveals no significant difference between the two groups in any case. The 'CR' value between the two groups for the 'r' of level of aspiration score with theoretical, economic, social, political, aesthetic and religious value dimensions are .73, .20, .13, .67, .47 and .33 respectively, which are not significant at .05 level. However, the table shows that the relationship of level of aspiration score and three value dimensions of male group namely, economic, social and political are slightly stronger than the female group. These are .09, .03 and -.09 respectively for male group and .06, .01, .01 respectively for female group. On the other hand, the relationship between level of aspiration score and remaining three value dimensions of female group namely, theoretical, aesthetic and religious are slightly stronger than the male group with 'r' of .27, -.10 and -.20 respectively for female group and .17, -.03 and -.15 respectively for the male group. Thus, no remarkable difference is observed in the relationship of level of aspiration score and value dimensions between male and female undergraduate students of technical professional courses. Hence, it may be inferred that level of aspiration exerts more or less similar type of influence upon the six value dimensions among both male and female students of technical professional courses. It can also be concluded that gender may not cause a significant variance in the nature of relationship between scores of level of aspiration and value dimensions of undergraduate students of technical professional courses.

Similar to the male and female of technical professional courses, the researcher has also compared the relationship of scores on level of aspiration and different value dimensions between male and female students of non-technical professional courses, which are presented in Table 4.31.

Table 4.31: Significance of Difference in the Relationship of scores on Level of Aspiration and each of the Six Value Dimensions between Male and Female Undergraduate Students of Non-Technical Professional Courses

Value Dimensions	*Male Students of Non-Technical Professional Courses (N=64)*		*Female Students of Non-Technical Professional Courses (N=79)*		*SE_{Diff} (Z)*	*CR*	*Status*
	r-value	*z-value*	*r-value*	*z-value*			
Theoretical	.03	.03	.25	.26	.17	1.35	NS
Economic	.36	.38	.26	.27	.17	.65	NS
Social	-.04	-.04	-.14	-.14	.17	.59	NS
Political	-.01	-.01	-.11	-.11	.17	.59	NS
Aesthetic	-.04	-.04	-.16	-.16	.17	.71	NS
Religious	-.29	-.30	-.14	-.14	.17	.94	NS

Note: S= Significant at .05 level; NS= Not Significant at .05 level.

The result contained in the Table 4.31 shows that there is no significant difference between male and female undergraduate students of non-technical professional courses in the relationship of scores on level of aspiration and value dimensions. The 'CR' value between the two groups for the 'r' of level of aspiration score with theoretical, economic, social, political, aesthetic and religious value dimensions are .73, .20, .13, .67, .47 and .33 respectively, which are not significant at .05 level. However, the table shows that the relationship of level of aspiration score and two value dimensions of male group namely, economic and religious are stronger than the female group with 'r' values of .36 and -.29 respectively for male group and .26 and -.14 respectively for female group. On the other hand, the relationship between level of aspiration score and remaining four value dimensions of female group are slightly stronger than the male group. These are namely, theoretical, social, political and aesthetic with 'r' of .25, -.14, -.11 and -.16 respectively for female group and .03, -.04, -.01 and -.04 respectively for the male group. Thus, no remarkable difference is observed in the relationship of scores on level of aspiration and value dimensions between male and female undergraduate students of non-technical professional courses. Hence, it may be inferred that level of aspiration exerts more or less similar type of influence upon the six value dimensions among both male and female students of non-technical professional courses. It can also be concluded that gender may not cause a significant variance in the nature of relationship between scores on level of aspiration and value dimensions of undergraduate students of non-technical professional courses.

The 'CR' test has also been employed in the 'r' values of scores on level of aspiration and different value dimensions between male undergraduate students of technical and non-technical professional courses, which are presented in Table 4.32.

Table 4.32: Significance of Difference in the Relationship of scores on Level of Aspiration and each of the Six Value Dimensions between Male Undergraduate Students of Technical and Non-Technical Professional Courses

Value Dimensions	*Male Students of Technical Professional Courses (N=138)*		*Male Students of Non-Technical Professional Courses (N=64)*		*SE_{Diff} (Z)*	*CR*	*Status*
	r-value	*z-value*	*r-value*	*z-value*			
Theoretical	.17	.17	.03	.03	.15	.93	NS
Economic	.09	.09	.36	.38	.15	1.93	NS
Social	.03	.03	-.04	-.04	.15	.47	NS
Political	-.09	-.09	-.01	-.01	.15	.53	NS
Aesthetic	-.03	-.03	-.04	-.04	.15	.07	NS
Religious	-.15	-.15	-.29	-.30	.15	1.0	NS

Note: S= Significant at .05 level; NS= Not Significant at .05 level.

The Table 4.32 shows that there is no significant difference between male undergraduate students of technical and non-technical professional courses in the relationship of scores on level of aspiration and value dimensions. The 'CR' value between the two groups for the 'r' of level of aspiration score with theoretical, economic, social, political, aesthetic and religious value dimensions are .93, 1.93, .47, .53, .07, and .33 respectively, which are not significant at .05 level. However, the table shows that the relationship of scores on level of aspiration and four value dimensions namely, economic, social, aesthetic and religious of male technical professional group are weaker than the male non-technical professional group with 'r' of .09, .03, -.03 and -.15 respectively for the former group and .38, -.04, -.04 and -.30 respectively for the later group. On the other hand, the relationship of scores on level of aspiration and two value dimensions of male technical professional group namely, theoretical and political are stronger than that of the male non-technical professional group with 'r' values of .17 and -.09 respectively for the former group and .03, and -.01 respectively for the later group. The maximum difference is observed between the two groups with regard to the relationship of level of aspiration and economic value dimension with 'CR' score of 1.93. The difference is slightly away from 1.96 to be significant at .05 confidence level. Thus, the difference between no two 'r's between the two groups reached the level of statistical significance at .05 level. Except economic value, all other 'r' values as well as differences between 'r' values as evident are generally not taken in to consideration and treated as very nominal and negligible. Hence, it may be inferred that level of aspiration exerts more or less similar type of influence upon the value dimensions among male undergraduate students of both technical and non-technical professional courses.

Table 4.33: Significance of Difference in the Relationship of scores on Level of Aspiration and each of the Six Value Dimensions between Female Undergraduate Students of Technical and Non-Technical Professional Courses

Value Dimensions	*Female Students of Technical Professional Courses (N=70)*		*Female Students of Non-Technical Professional Courses (N=79)*		*SE_{Diff} (Z)*	*CR*	*Status*
	r-value	*z-value*	*r-value*	*z-value*			
Theoretical	.27	.28	.25	.26	.17	.12	NS
Economic	.06	.06	.26	.27	.17	1.24	NS
Social	.01	.01	-.14	-.14	.17	.88	NS
Political	.01	.01	-.11	-.11	.17	.71	NS
Aesthetic	-.10	-.10	-.16	-.16	.17	.35	NS
Religious	-.20	-.20	-.14	-.14	.17	.35	NS

Note: S= Significant at .05 level; NS= Not Significant at .05 level.

The investigator has also employed the 'CR' test in 'r' values of scores on level of aspiration and different value dimensions between female undergraduate students of technical and non-technical professional courses, which are presented in Table 4.33.

The Table 4.33 reveals that there is no significant difference between female undergraduate students of technical and non-technical professional courses in the relationship of scores on level of aspiration and value dimensions. The 'CR' value between the two groups for the 'r' of level of aspiration score with theoretical, economic, social, political, aesthetic and religious value dimensions are .12, 1.24, .88, .71, .35, and .35 respectively, which are not significant at .05 level. However, the table shows that the correlation of level of aspiration scores with two value dimensions of female technical professional group namely, theoretical and religious are slightly higher than that of the female non-technical professional group with 'r' values of .27 and -.20 respectively for the former group and .25, and -.14 respectively for the later group. On the other hand, the correlations of level of aspiration score with remaining four value dimensions of female technical professional group are lower than the female non-technical professional group. These are economic, social, political and aesthetic values with 'r' of .06, .01, .01 and -.10 respectively for the former group and .26, -.14, -.11 and -.16 respectively for the later group. The maximum difference is observed between the two groups with regard to the relationship of level of aspiration score and economic value dimension with 'CR' score of 1.23. Thus, the difference between no two 'r's between the two groups reached the level of statistical significance at .05 level. Except economic value, all other 'r' values as well as differences between 'r' values as evident are generally not taken in to consideration and treated as very nominal and negligible. Hence, it may be inferred that level of aspiration exerts more or less similar type of influence upon the value dimensions among female undergraduate students of both technical and non-technical professional courses.

Thus, the comparison of the relationship between the two variables reveals that the differences in the correlations of level of aspiration score with all the six value dimensions are statistically insignificant at .05 level between undergraduate students of technical and non-technical professional courses; between male and female undergraduate students of professional courses, between male and female students of technical as well as non-technical professional courses, and between male as well as female students of technical and non-technical professional courses. Thus, it is perceived that nature of course as well as gender may not affect the relationship between score on level of aspiration and each of the six value dimensions.

Objective-8: *To study the level of aspiration as predictor of value dimensions of undergraduate students of both technical and non-technical professional courses.*

H_7 : *Level of aspiration is the predictor of value dimensions of undergraduate students of both technical and non-technical professional courses.*

In order to answer the last objective of the study, linear regression coefficient is computed and regression equations of level of aspiration as predictor of each of the six value dimensions are set up separately for students of technical and non-technical professional courses. The equations thus obtained are presented in table 4.34, along with the standard errors of estimates and coefficients of forecasting efficiency. Y in all the equations refers to criterion or dependent variable i.e. Value Dimensions and X refers to the predictor variable i.e. Level of Aspiration.

Table 4.34: Linear Regression Equations with their Standard Errors of Estimate and Coefficients of Forecasting Efficiency for Predicting Value Dimensions of Undergraduate Students of Technical and Non-Technical Professional Courses

Value Dimensions	*Students of Technical Professional Courses (N=208)*			*Students of Non-Technical Professional Courses (N=143)*		
	Equations	$SE_{(est)}$	*E in %*	*Equations*	$SE_{(est)}$	*E in %*
Theoretical	Y= 42.874 + .638X	5.830	2.08	Y= 41.425 + .537X	4.670	1.32
Economic	Y= 43.452 + .277X	6.102	.37	Y= 39.864 + 1.166X	5.870	3.8
Social	Y= 37.825 + .061X	5.779	.02	Y= 40.322 - .322X	6.079	.28
Political	Y= 40.147 - .115X	5.082	.09	Y= 41.275 - .363X	4.918	.55
Aesthetic	Y= 38.274 - .195X	6.182	.18	Y= 38.913 - .232X	5.326	.19
Religious	Y= 37.401 - .654X	7.468	1.35	Y= 38.210 - .854X	6.010	2.0

The Table 4.34 depicting the regression equation of level of aspiration, standard errors of the estimates and coefficients of forecasting efficiency for predicting each of the six value dimensions of undergraduate students of technical and non-technical professional students shows that level of aspiration is positive predictor of three value dimensions of students of technical professional courses. These are theoretical, economic and social, while negative predictor of the remaining three value dimensions i.e. political, aesthetic and religious. So far the students of non-technical professional courses are concerned, level of aspiration has turned out as positive predictor of two value dimensions i.e. theoretical and economic, while negative for remaining four value dimensions. Further, the table reveals that every unit increase in level of aspiration score accompanies an increase of .638, .277 and .061 units in theoretical, economic and social value respectively, and a decrease of .115, .195 and .654 units in the scores of political, aesthetic and religious value respectively for the students of technical professional courses. Similarly, so far the students of non-technical professional courses are concerned, it is observed that every unit increase in level of aspiration score accompanies an increase of .537 and 1.166 units in theoretical and economic value respectively, while social, political, aesthetic and religious value decreases by .322, .363, .232 and .854 units respectively. As such H_7 stating ***"level of aspiration is the predictor of value dimensions of undergraduate students of both technical and non-technical professional courses"*** is accepted for both the groups.

Thus, it become clear that level of aspiration contributes most towards religious followed by theoretical value dimension and least towards social followed by political value of students of technical professional courses, whereas it contributes most towards economic followed by religious value and least towards aesthetic followed by social value for students of non-technical professional courses.

The Table 4.34 further reveals that the values of coefficients of forecasting efficiency ranged between .02 to 2.08 percent for the six value dimensions of students of technical professional courses. The highest forecasting efficiency coefficient i.e. 2.08 per cent is documented for theoretical value and lowest for social value. This implies that the prediction of theoretical value by level of aspiration is most efficient and social value is least efficient. The prediction of theoretical value by level of aspiration as mentioned earlier is only 2.08 per cent efficient or it can be said that the prediction of theoretical value by level of aspiration using the equation *"Theortical Value (Y) = 42.874 + .638X (Level of Aspiration)"* is 2.08 per cent less error than the prediction made merely from the knowledge of mean scores of criterion and predictor variable so far the students of technical professional courses are concerned, which is regarded as quite low level of efficiency. It is worth mentioning that forecasting efficiency coefficients of the remaining five value dimensions are much lower than that of theoretical value. Only .37 per cent, .02 per cent, .09 per cent, .18 per cent and 1.35 per cent forecasting efficiency for the regression equations of level of aspiration on economic, social, political, aesthetic and religious values respectively are recorded, implying that the prediction of these value dimensions by level of aspiration through using the regression equations mentioned in table 4.34 are poorly efficient so far the students of technical professional courses are concerned.

On the other hand, coefficients of forecasting efficiency ranged between .19 to 3.8 per cent for the six value dimensions of students of non-technical professional courses. The maximum efficiency (*E*) i.e. 3.8 per cent is for economic value and minimum i.e. .19 for aesthetic value. Thus, it can be implied that the prediction of economic value by level of aspiration is most efficient and aesthetic value is least efficient out of the six value dimensions. The regression equation of level of aspiration on economic value is 3.8 per cent efficient or it can be said that the prediction of theoretical value by level of aspiration of students of non-technical courses using the equation mentioned in Table 4.34 is 3.8 per cent less error than those made merely from the knowledge of mean scores of criterion and predictor variable. On the other hand, the forecasting efficiency coefficients of other five value dimensions are found not exceeding even two per cent. 1.32 per cent, .28 per cent, .55 per cent, .19 per cent and 2.0 per cent forecasting efficiency coefficients are recorded for the regression equation of level of aspiration on theoretical, social, political, aesthetic and religious value dimensions respectively. Thus, poor efficiency level is documented for the prediction of value dimensions by level of aspiration of students of non-technical professional courses.

In the pertinent, it can be concluded that level of aspiration is a poor predictor of all the six value dimensions of students of both technical and non-technical professional courses.

In order to know the predicting nature of level of aspiration on value dimensions of male and female students of professional courses, linear regression coefficient is computed and regression equations of level of aspiration as predictor of each of the six value dimensions are set up separately for both the groups. The equations thus obtained are presented in Table 4.35, along with the standard errors of estimates and coefficients of forecasting efficiency. Y in all the equations refers to criterion or dependent variable i.e. Value Dimensions and X refers to the predictor variable i.e. Level of Aspiration.

Table 4.35: Linear Regression Equations with their Standard Errors of Estimate and Coefficients of Forecasting Efficiency for Predicting Value Dimensions of Male and Female Undergraduate Students of Professional Courses

Value Dimensions	*Male Students of Professional Courses (N=202)*			*Female Students of Professional Courses (N=149)*		
	Equations	$SE_{(est)}$	*E in %*	*Equations*	$SE_{(est)}$	*E in %*
Theoretical	Y= 42.301 + .614X	5.755	1.78	Y= 41.484 + .852X	5.006	2.61
Economic	Y= 42.933 + .527X	6.004	1.22	Y= 40.882 + .617X	6.008	1.47
Social	Y= 38.140 - .023X	6.320	.002	Y= 40.079 - .242X	5.308	.30
Political	Y= 42.036 - .312X	4.796	.68	Y= 38.969 - .145X	4.939	.13
Aesthetic	Y= 36.702 - .028X	5.753	.004	Y= 40.954 - .444X	5.509	.92
Religious	Y= 37.789 - .750X	7.227	1.69	Y= 37.642 - .684X	6.466	1.56

The result of the regression equations presented in Table 4.35 reveals that level of aspiration is positive predictor of two value dimensions of both male and female undergraduate students of professional courses. These are theoretical and economic; while it is negative predictor of the remaining four value dimensions namely, social, political, aesthetic and religious for both the groups. It is found that every unit increase in level of aspiration accompanies an increase of .614 and .527 units in theoretical and economic value respectively, while decreases by .023, .312, .028 and .750 units in social, political, aesthetic and religious value respectively for male group. On the other hand, for the female group it is found that every unit increase in level of aspiration corresponds an increase of .852 and .617 units in theoretical and economic value respectively, while social, political, aesthetic and religious value decreases by .242, .145, .444 and 684 units respectively.

Thus, it can be inferred that level of aspiration contributes most towards religious followed by theoretical value and least towards social followed by aesthetic value of male undergraduate students of professional courses. On the other hand, it contributes most towards theoretical followed by religious value and least towards political followed by social value of the female students of professional courses.

The prediction of all the six value dimensions by level of aspiration for both male and female undergraduate students of professional courses as mentioned in Table 4.35 are found not much error free or efficient enough as revealed by the values of coefficients of forecasting efficiency. So far the male group is concerned, out of the six values the maximum forecasting efficiency coefficient i.e. 1.78 per cent is recorded for the regression equation of level of aspiration on theoretical value. This implies that the prediction of theoretical value by level of aspiration using the regression equation "Y= 42.301 + .614X" (where X= Level of aspiration and Y= Theoretical value) as mentioned in Table 4.35 is only 1.78 per cent efficient. Simply, it can be said that chances of error in the prediction of theoretical value by level of aspiration of male group is 98.22 out of 100. The value of forecasting efficiency of regression equations of level of aspiration on remaining five value dimensions of male group are further nominal as found in Table 4.35.

Similarly, with regard to the female group also the maximum forecasting efficiency coefficient is found for the regression equation of level of aspiration on theoretical value with E value of 2.61 per cent. That means, the prediction of theoretical value by level of aspiration for female group is 2.61 per cent efficient or the chances of errors in prediction is 97.39 out of 100. Further, the coefficients of forecasting efficiency for equations of level of aspiration on remaining five value dimensions are found not exceeding even 1.56 per cent for female students of professional courses. Thus, level of aspiration is a poor predictor of all the value dimensions of both male and female undergraduate students of professional courses.

Linear regression coefficient and regression equations of level of aspiration as predictor of each of the six value dimensions are also set up separately for male and female students of technical professional courses, which are presented in Table 4.36. Y in all the equations refers to criterion or dependent variable i.e. Value Dimensions and X refers to the predictor variable i.e. Level of Aspiration.

Table 4.36: Linear Regression Equations with their Standard Errors of Estimate and Coefficients of Forecasting Efficiency for Predicting Value Dimensions of Male and Female Undergraduate Students of Technical Professional Courses.

Value Dimensions	*Male Students of Technical Professional Courses (N=138)*			*Female Students of Technical Professional Courses (N=70)*		
	Equations	$SE_{(est)}$	*E (%)*	*Equations*	$SE_{(est)}$	*E (%)*
Theoretical	Y= 43.166 + .545X	6.035	1.49	Y= 42.256 + .852X	5.468	3.83
Economic	Y= 43.742 + .289X	6.053	.42	Y= 43.057 + .195X	6.232	.16
Social	Y= 37.420 + .098X	5.844	.05	Y= 38.492 + .025X	5.689	.03
Political	Y= 41.200 - .224X	4.843	.40	Y= 38.385 + .018X	5.326	.004
Aesthetic	Y= 37.228 - .088X	6.097	.04	Y= 40.020 - .323X	6.205	.45
Religious	Y= 37.232 - .608X	7.814	1.12	Y= 37.745 - .757X	6.838	1.98

Level of aspiration is positive predictor of three value dimensions namely, theoretical, economic and social; while it is negative predictor of the remaining three value dimensions namely, political, aesthetic and religious of male undergraduate students of technical professional courses as evident from the regression equations presented in Table 4.6. So far the female students of technical professional courses are concerned, the table reveals that level of aspiration has positively predicted four value dimensions namely, theoretical, economic, social and political, while negatively predicted the remaining two value dimensions i.e. aesthetic and religious. With regard to male group, the table further reveals that every unit increase in level of aspiration accompanies an increase of .545, .289 and .098 units in theoretical, economic and social value respectively, while decreases by .224, .088 and .607 units in political, aesthetic and religious value respectively. On the other hand, for the female it is found that every unit increase in level of aspiration accompanies an increase of .852, .195, .025 and .018 units in theoretical, economic, social and political value respectively, while aesthetic and religious value decreases by .323 and .757 units respectively. In this way, it is clear that level of aspiration contributes most towards religious followed by theoretical value dimension and least towards aesthetic followed by social value of male undergraduate students of technical professional courses, whereas it contributes most towards theoretical followed by religious value and least towards political followed by social value dimension of the female students of technical professional courses. This result of prediction of value dimensions by level of aspiration of male and female students of technical professional courses is similar to that of the prediction made for male and female students of professional courses as a whole except the two least predicted values of malc group. Thcsc arc found social followed by aesthetic for former group, while aesthetic followed by social for the later group.

However, the result of coefficients of forecasting efficiency shows that the prediction of all the six value dimensions of both male and female undergraduate students of technical professional courses as mentioned in Table 4.36 are not efficient enough. So far the male group is concerned, out of the six values the maximum forecasting efficiency coefficient i.e. 1.49 per cent, is recorded for the regression equation of level of aspiration on theoretical value. This implies that the prediction of theoretical value by level of aspiration as mentioned in Table 4.36 is only 1.49 per cent efficient, or it can be said that chances of error in the prediction of theoretical value by level of aspiration of male group is 99.51 out of 100. The value of forecasting efficiency of regression equations of level of aspiration on remaining five value dimensions of male group are found further lower. Similarly, with regard to the female group, the maximum forecasting efficiency coefficient is found for the regression equation of level of aspiration on theoretical value with E value of 3.83 per cent. That means, the prediction of theoretical value by level of aspiration for female group is 3.83 per cent efficient or the chances of error in prediction is 96.17 out of 100. The coefficients of forecasting efficiency for equations of level of aspiration on remaining five value dimensions of female group has not exceeded even 2 per cent. Thus, in the pertinent of the analysis of the regression equations of level of aspiration along with their coefficients of forecasting efficiency, it can be concluded that level of aspiration is a poor predictor of all the value dimensions of both male and female undergraduate students of technical professional courses.

Linear regression coefficient and regression equations of level of aspiration as predictor of each of the six value dimensions are also set up separately for male and female students of non-technical professional courses, which are presented in Table 4.37. Y in all the equations refers to criterion or dependent variable i.e. Value Dimensions and X refers to the predictor variable i.e. Level of Aspiration.

Table 4.37: Linear Regression Equations with their Standard Errors of Estimate and Coefficients of Forecasting Efficiency for Predicting Value Dimensions of Male and Female Undergraduate Students of Non-Technical Professional Courses.

Value Dimensions	*Male Students of Non-Technical Professional Courses (N=64)*			*Female Students of Non-Technical Professional Courses (N=79)*		
	Equations	$SE_{(est)}$	*E (%)*	*Equations*	$SE_{(est)}$	*E (%)*
Theoretical	Y= 42.190 + .108X	4.874	.04	Y= 41.130 + .730X	4.514	3.05
Economic	Y= 39.862 + 1.788X	5.743	6.78	Y= 39.098 + .996X	5.702	3.52
Social	Y= 39.302 - .226X	7.286	.08	Y= 41.304 - .449X	4.893	1.01
Political	Y= 42.506 - .034X	4.536	.004	Y= 39.540 - .332X	4.620	.62
Aesthetic	Y= 36.338 - .164X	4.943	.08	Y= 41.607 - .505X	4.832	1.30
Religious	Y= 39.529 – 1.398X	5.805	2.63	Y= 37.459 - .575X	6.200	1.03

So far the prediction of value dimensions of male and female undergraduate students of non-technical professional courses are concerned, the Table 4.37 shows that level of aspiration is positive predictor of two value dimensions of both male and female students of non-technical professional courses. These are theoretical and economic, while negative predictor of the remaining four values namely, social, political, aesthetic and religious for both the groups. Moreover, it is noted that every unit increase in level of aspiration accompanies an increase of .108 and 1.788 units in theoretical and economic value respectively, and a decrease of .226, .034, .164 and 1.398 units in social, political, aesthetic and religious value respectively for the male students of non-technical professional courses. Similarly, with regard to the female group, every unit increase in level of aspiration accompanies an increase of .730 and .996 units in theoretical and economic value respectively, whereas social, political, aesthetic and religious value decreases by .449, .332, .505 and .575 units respectively. Thus, it become clear that level of aspiration contributes most towards economic value and least towards political value dimension of both male and female students of non-technical professional courses.

The Table 4.37 further reveals that the values of coefficients of forecasting efficiency ranged between .04 to 6.78 per cent for the regression equations of level of aspiration on the six value dimensions of male students and between .62 to 3.52 per cent for the regression equations of level of aspiration on the six values of female students of non-technical professional courses. The highest forecasting efficiency coefficient is found for equation on economic value dimension for both the groups. These are 6.78 per cent and 3.52 per cent respectively for male and female group. This implies that the prediction of economic value by level of aspiration on the basis of regression equations mentioned in table 4.37 is 6.78 per cent efficient for male group and 3.52 per cent efficient for female group. The chances of error in prediction of economic value by level of aspiration are 93.32 per cent for male group and 96.48 per cent for female group of non-technical professional courses. Similar inference can be made with regard to the strength of prediction of remaining five value dimensions of both the groups on the basis of their respective scores of forecasting efficiency coefficients, which shows that level of aspiration is relatively a poor predictor of all the value dimensions of both male and female undergraduate students of non-technical professional courses.

The investigator has also computed linear regression coefficient and set up regression equations of level of aspiration as predictor of each of the six value dimensions separately for male students of technical and non-technical professional courses, which are presented in Table 4.38. Y in all the equations refers to criterion or dependent variable i.e. Value Dimensions and X refers to the predictor variable i.e. Level of Aspiration.

Table 4.38: Linear Regression Equations with their Standard Errors of Estimate and Coefficients of Forecasting Efficiency for Predicting Value Dimensions of Male Undergraduate Students of Technical and Non-Technical Professional Courses

Value Dimensions	*Male Students of Technical Professional Courses (N=138)*			*Male Students of Non-Technical Professional Courses (N=64)*		
	Equations	$SE_{(est)}$	*E (%)*	*Equations*	$SE_{(est)}$	*E(%)*
Theoretical	Y= 43.166 + .545X	6.035	1.49	Y= 42.190 + .108X	4.874	.04
Economic	Y= 43.742 + .289X	6.053	.42	Y= 39.862 + 1.788X	5.743	6.78
Social	Y= 37.420 + .098X	5.844	.05	Y= 39.302 - .226X	7.286	.08
Political	Y= 41.200 - .224X	4.843	.40	Y= 42.506 - .034X	4.536	.004
Aesthetic	Y= 37.228 - .088X	6.097	.04	Y= 36.338 - .164X	4.943	.08
Religious	Y= 37.232 - .608X	7.814	1.12	Y= 39.529 – 1.398X	5.805	2.63

Level of aspiration is positive predictor of three value dimensions namely, theoretical, economic and social, while negative predictor of the remaining three values namely, political, aesthetic and religious of male undergraduate students of technical professional courses as evident from the regression equations presented in Table 4.38. On the other hand, it is positive predictor of two value dimensions namely, theoretical and economic, while negative predictor of the remaining four values namely, social, political, aesthetic and religious of male students of non-technical professional courses.

With regard to male group of technical professional courses, the table further reveals that every unit increase in level of aspiration accompanies an increase of .545, .289 and .098 units in theoretical, economic and social value respectively, while decreases by .224, .088 and .607 units in political, aesthetic and religious value respectively.

On the other hand, with regard to male group of non-technical professional courses, it is noted that every unit increase in level of aspiration accompanies an increase of .108 and 1.788 units in theoretical and economic value respectively, and a decrease of .226, .034, .164 and 1.398 units in social, political, aesthetic and religious value respectively. In this way, it is clear that level of aspiration contributes most towards religious followed by theoretical value and least towards aesthetic value of male undergraduate students of technical professional courses, whereas it contributes most towards economic followed by religious value and least towards political value of male undergraduate students of non-technical professional courses.

So far the male group of technical professional courses is concerned, the values of coefficients of forecasting efficiency shows that out of the six value dimensions the maximum forecasting efficiency coefficient i.e. 1.49 per cent, is recorded for the regression equation of level of aspiration on theoretical value. This implies that the prediction of theoretical value by level of aspiration as mentioned in Table 4.38 is only 1.49 per cent efficient, or it can be said that chances of error in the prediction of theoretical value by level of aspiration of male students of technical professional courses is 99.51 out of 100. The value of forecasting efficiency of regression equation of level of aspiration on remaining five value dimensions of male students of technical courses are much lower as presented in Table 4.38. Again, the values of coefficients of forecasting efficiency ranged between .04 to 6.78 per cent for the equations of level of aspiration on the six value dimensions of male students of non-technical professional courses. The highest forecasting efficiency coefficient is found for regression equation of level of aspiration on economic value dimension i.e. 6.78 per cent. This implies that the prediction of economic value by level of aspiration on the basis of regression equation presented in Table 4.38 is 6.78 per cent efficient. The chance of error in prediction of economic value by level of aspiration is 93.32 out of 100. The forecasting efficiency of equations of level of aspiration on remaining five value dimensions of male students of non-technical professional courses are found much lower even than that of the economic value. Thus, it is observed that the predictions of all the six value dimensions of male undergraduate students of both technical and non-technical professional courses are not much error free or not efficient enough. Hence, level of aspiration proves a poor predictor of all the value dimensions of male undergraduate students of both technical and non-technical professional courses.

Linear regression coefficient and regression equations of level of aspiration as predictor of each of the six value dimensions are also set up separately for male undergraduate students of technical and non-technical professional courses, which are presented in Table 4.39. Y in all the equations refers to criterion or dependent variable i.e. Value Dimensions and X refers to the predictor variable i.e. Level of Aspiration.

Table 4.39: Linear Regression Equations with their Standard Errors of Estimate and Coefficients of Forecasting Efficiency for Predicting Value Dimensions of Female Undergraduate Students of Technical and Non-Technical Professional Courses.

Value Dimensions	*Female Students of Technical Professional Courses (N=70)*			*Female Students of Non-Technical Professional Courses (N=79)*		
	Equations	$SE_{(est)}$	*E (%)*	*Equations*	$SE_{(est)}$	*E (%)*
Theoretical	Y= 42.256 + .852X	5.468	3.83	Y= 41.130 + .730X	4.514	3.05
Economic	Y= 43.057 + .195X	6.232	.16	Y= 39.098 + .996X	5.702	3.52
Social	Y= 38.492 + .025X	5.689	.03	Y= 41.304 - .449X	4.893	1.01
Political	Y= 38.385 + .018X	5.326	.004	Y= 39.540 - .332X	4.620	.62
Aesthetic	Y= 40.020 - .323X	6.205	.45	Y= 41.607 - .505X	4.832	1.30
Religious	Y= 37.745 - .757X	6.838	1.98	Y= 37.459 - .575X	6.200	1.03

The result of regression equations presented in Table 4.39 reveals that level of aspiration is positive predictor of four value dimensions namely, theoretical, economic, social and political, while negative predictor of aesthetic and religious value dimensions of the female students of technical professional courses. On the other hand, level of aspiration is positive predictor of theoretical and economic value dimensions, and negative predictor of remaining four value dimensions namely, social, political, aesthetic and religious of female students of non-technical professional courses.

Moreover, with regard to female group of technical professional courses, the table shows that every unit increase in level of aspiration accompanies an increase of .852, .195, .025 and .018 units in theoretical, economic, social and political value respectively, while aesthetic and religious value decreases by .323, and .757 units respectively. On the other hand, with regard to the female group of non-technical professional courses it is noted that every unit increase in level of aspiration accompanies an increase of .730 and .996 units in theoretical and economic value respectively, whereas social, political, aesthetic and religious value decreases by .449, .332, .505 and .575 units respectively. Thus, it became clear that level of aspiration contributes most towards theoretical followed by religious value and least towards political followed by social value of the female students of technical professional courses. On the other hand, it contributes most towards economic followed by theoretical value and least towards political followed by social value of female students of non-technical professional courses.

The Table 4.39 further reveals that the values of coefficients of forecasting efficiency ranged between .004 to 3.83 per cent for the regression equations of level of aspiration on the six value dimensions of female students of technical professional courses and between .62 to 3.52 per cent for female students of non-technical professional courses. The maximum forecasting efficiency coefficient is found for the regression equation of level of aspiration on theoretical value with E of 3.83 per cent for females of technical professional courses. That means, the prediction of theoretical value by level of aspiration for female students of technical professional courses is 3.83 per cent efficient or the chances of error in prediction is 96.17 out of 100. Similarly, the highest forecasting efficiency coefficient is found for equation on economic value dimension for female group of non-technical professional courses with E of 3.52 per cent. This implies that the prediction of economic value by level of aspiration on the basis of regression equation mentioned in Table 4.39 is 3.52 per cent efficient for female students of non-technical professional courses. The chances of error in prediction of economic value by level of aspiration are 96.48 per cent. Similar inference can be drawn with regard to the strength of predictions of remaining five value dimensions of both the groups on the basis of their respective scores of forecasting efficiency coefficients, which shows that level of aspiration is a poor predictor of all the value dimensions of female undergraduate students of both technical and non-technical professional courses.

The linear regression coefficient and regression equations of level of aspiration as predictor of each of the six value dimensions are set up for undergraduate students of professional courses as a whole, which are presented in Table 4.40. Y in all the equations refers to criterion or dependent variable i.e. Value Dimensions and X refers to the predictor variable i.e. Level of Aspiration.

Table 4.40: Linear Regression Equations with their Standard Errors of Estimate and Coefficients of Forecasting Efficiency for Predicting Value Dimensions of Undergraduate Students of Professional Courses

Value Dimensions	*Undergraduate Students of Professional Courses (N=351)*		
	Equations	$SE_{(est)}$	*E in %*
Theoretical	Y= 41.961 + .709X	5.439	2.52
Economic	Y= 41.988 + .589X	6.053	1.42
Social	Y= 39.009 - .128X	5.933	.07
Political	Y= 40.629 - .209X	5.009	.27
Aesthetic	Y= 38.619 - .236X	5.838	.25
Religious	Y= 37.732 - .725X	6.895	1.65

So far the prediction of value dimensions of undergraduate students of professional courses irrespective of their gender and nature of course is concerned, Table 4.40 shows that level of aspiration is positive predictor of theoretical and economic value dimensions, while negative predictor of the remaining four value dimensions namely, social, political, aesthetic and religious. Further, it is noted that every unit increase in level of aspiration corresponds an increase of .709 and .589 units in theoretical and economic value respectively, whereas social, political, aesthetic and religious value decreases by .128, .209, .236 and .725 units respectively. Thus, it can be said that level of aspiration contributes most towards religious value (negatively) followed by theoretical value (positively), whereas least towards social followed by political value (both negatively) of undergraduate students of professional courses.

However, the result of coefficients of forecasting efficiency reveals that the prediction of all the six value dimensions by level of aspiration are not much error free or not much efficient. It is found that the maximum value of forecasting efficiency i.e. 2.52 per cent is recorded for the regression equation of level of aspiration on theoretical value dimension, which implies that the prediction of theoretical value by level of aspiration is only 2.52 per cent efficient, or the chances of error in the prediction is 97.48 per cent. The forecasting efficiency coefficient of the regression equations of level of aspiration on the remaining five value dimensions has not exceeded even 1.65 per cent. Thus, it can be concluded that level of aspiration is a poor predictor of all the six value dimensions of undergraduate students of professional courses.

The foregoing analysis of the regression equations of level of aspiration on value dimensions of different groups of samples shows that level of aspiration is a variable that contributes most towards religious, theoretical and economic value dimensions in almost all the cases. The two value dimensions that are contributed most by level of aspiration in case of students of technical professional courses are religious followed by theoretical. When analysis is made separately on male and female students of the same course i.e. technical professional courses, it is found that in case of male group this order remains intact to that of the total group, while in case of female group the order of the two values has changed. With regard to the least predicted value dimension, minor divergence is observed. Social followed by political value are least contributed by level of aspiration for the total group, while these are aesthetic followed by social for the male group and political followed by social for female group of technical professional courses.

Again, so far the students of non-technical professional courses are concerned, the analysis has revealed that economic followed by religious values are most contributed by level of aspiration. A gender-wise analysis reveals almost similar type of results. Economic followed by religious remained the two most contributed value dimensions in case of male group of non-technical professional courses. Variance is observed in case of female group where economic followed by theoretical value are the two most contributed value dimensions. On the other hand, the least contributed value dimension of both male and female students of non-technical professional courses is found political.

Thus, it is observed that though order changed; theoretical, religious and economic value dimensions are most contributed by level of aspiration in all the cases. Religious and theoretical value remain prominent in both male and female of technical group, whereas economic, religious and theoretical remain prominent in case of non-technical professional group of which economic and religious for males and economic and theoretical for females. The finding reported by Ranu, Sarbjit Kaur (1995) also goes in line of the finding of the present study, who revealed that level of aspiration contributes most towards the prediction of religious value of male group and theoretical value of female group of post-graduate students.

Though, more or less, level of aspiration contributes in the prediction of all the six value dimensions of all groups of samples, the forecasting efficiency coefficient of no regression equation is found to exceed 6.78 per cent. Thus, it is understood that the prediction of all the six value dimensions of different groups of samples using the regression equations mentioned from Tables 4.34 to 4.40 would not be much error free. Hence, it can be concluded that level of aspiration is a poor predictor of value dimensions of undergraduate students of professional courses.

In this way, this Chapter IV includes the data, their statistical analysis, interpretation and discussion in consonance with the need of the study so as to satisfy the pre-formulated research questions. The foregoing chapter comprises analysis related to the magnitude of scores on different value dimensions as well as level of aspiration in different target groups, involving a comparison among these groups with regard to value dimensions as well as level of aspiration score; magnitude of relationship between value dimensions and level of aspiration in different target groups and comparison of these relationships among different target groups; prediction of value dimensions by level of aspiration through setting up of regression equations and determination of coefficients of forecasting efficiency of regression equations for different target groups. The different target groups taken in to consideration are undergraduate students of technical and non-technical professional courses; male and female undergraduate students of professional courses; male and female undergraduate students of technical professional courses; and male and female undergraduate students of non-technical professional courses. As such, the objectives of the study are fulfilled and hypotheses are tested and reflected in the interpretations made therein.

Chapter - V

Findings, Suggestions and Conclusion

The present chapter depicts the summary of major findings of the study followed by educational implications and suggestions, suggestions for further research in the related area and conclusion. The chapter ends with a brief summary of the report to enable a bird's eye view of it.

5.1. Major Findings of the Study

The summaries of major findings of the study are presented as follows:

(1) The order of preference of value dimensions of undergraduate students of technical professional courses is theoretical, followed by economic, political, social, aesthetic and religious which is economic followed by theoretical, political, social, aesthetic and religious for students of non-technical professional courses. Thus, except the two most preferred value dimensions, the preference order of remaining four value dimensions is same between the two groups.

(2) The order of preference of value dimensions of male undergraduate students of professional courses is economic followed by theoretical, political, social, aesthetic and religious whereas this order is theoretical followed by economic, aesthetic, social, political and religious for the female undergraduate students of professional courses. Thus, divergence is observed in the two most preferred value dimensions as well as in third and fifth preferred value

dimensions between male and female undergraduate students of professional courses. The two most preferred values of the male group are economic followed by theoretical, whereas with respect of female group the order has reversed. Similar case is observed with regard to the third and fifth preferred value dimensions, which are political and economic respectively for male group, whereas economic and political for the female group.

(3) The order of preference of value dimensions of male undergraduate students of technical professional courses is theoretical followed by economic, political, social, aesthetic and religious, whereas this order is theoretical followed by economic, aesthetic, social, political and religious for the female undergraduate students of technical professional courses. Thus, divergence is observed in the third and fifth preferred values between male and female undergraduate students of technical professional courses which are political and aesthetic respectively for the male group, whereas these are reverse in case of female group.

(4) The order of preference of value dimensions of male undergraduate students of non-technical professional courses is economic followed by theoretical, political, social, religious and aesthetic, whereas this order is theoretical followed by economic, aesthetic, social, political and religious for the female undergraduate students of non-technical professional courses. Thus, maximum divergence is observed in the preference order of value dimensions between male and female undergraduate students of non-technical professional courses. Except the social value that is placed at fourth position by both male and female group, the ranking order of other five values varied between the two groups.

(5) The preference order of value dimensions of male undergraduate students of technical professional courses is theoretical followed by economic, political, social, aesthetic and religious, whereas this order is economic followed by theoretical, political, social, religious and aesthetic for the male undergraduates of non-technical professional courses.

Thus, divergence is observed in the two most as well as two least preferred value dimensions between male undergraduate students of technical and non-technical professional courses.

(6) The order of preference of value dimensions of female undergraduate students of both technical and non-technical professional courses is theoretical followed by economic, aesthetic, social, and religious. Thus, no variance is found in the preference order of value dimensions between female undergraduate students of technical and non-technical professional courses.

(7) The order of preference of value dimensions of undergraduate students of professional courses is theoretical followed by economic, political, social, aesthetic and religious with mean scores of 44.11, 43.77, 39.99, 38.62, 37.90 and 35.53 respectively.

(8) Theoretical and economic values are the two most preferred value dimensions of all the target groups irrespective of the type of Course (Technical and Non-technical professional) and Gender. Theoretical and economic value dimensions are given first and second preference respectively by all the target groups, except the male group of non-technical professional courses who placed theoretical value at second place just after economic value.

(9) Irrespective of type of course and gender, the least preferred value of all the target groups is found religious except the male group of non-technical professional courses who gave religious value fifth preference.

(10) Social value is given fourth preference by all the target groups irrespective of type of course and gender.

(11) The preference order of value dimensions of female group of all categories i.e. females of professional courses; females of technical professional courses as well as non-technical professional courses remain same. This order is theoretical followed by economic, aesthetic, social, political and religious.

(12) There is significant difference between undergraduate students of technical and non-technical professional courses with

respect to three value dimensions namely, theoretical, economic and social. The students of technical professional courses scored significantly higher than their non-technical counterparts in theoretical and economic value dimensions, while the later group scored significantly higher than the former group in social value. No significant difference is found between the two groups with respect to the remaining three value dimensions namely, political, aesthetic and religious.

(13) There is significant difference between male and female undergraduate students of professional courses with respect to four value dimensions namely, economic, social, political and aesthetic. Male group is significantly higher in economic and political value dimensions than their female counterparts, while the female group is significantly higher in social and aesthetic value dimensions than the male counterparts. No significant difference is found between male and female undergraduate students of professional courses with respect to theoretical and religious value dimensions.

(14) There is significant difference between male and female undergraduate students of technical professional courses with respect to two value dimensions namely, political and aesthetic. Male group is significantly higher in political value than their female counterparts, while the female group is significantly higher in aesthetic value than their male counterparts. No significant difference is found between male and female undergraduate students of technical professional courses with respect to theoretical, economic, social and religious value dimensions.

(15) There is significant difference between male and female undergraduate students of non-technical professional courses with respect to three value dimensions namely, economic, political and aesthetic. Male group is significantly higher in economic and political value than their female counterparts, while the female group is significantly higher in aesthetic value than their male counterparts. No significant difference is found between male and female undergraduate students of

non-technical professional courses with respect to theoretical, social and religious value dimensions.

(16) There is significant difference between male undergraduate students of technical and non-technical professional courses with respect to two value dimensions namely, theoretical and political. Male students of technical professional courses are significantly higher in theoretical value dimension than male students of non-technical professional courses, while the later group is significantly higher in political value dimension than the former group. No significant difference is found between male undergraduate students of technical and non-technical professional courses with respect to economic, social, aesthetic and religious value dimensions.

(17) There is significant difference between female undergraduate students of technical and non-technical professional courses in theoretical value dimension, where the former group is significantly higher than the later group. No significant difference is found between female undergraduate students of technical and non-technical professional courses with respect to economic, social, political, aesthetic and religious value dimensions.

(18) 28.9 per cent, 38.5 per cent and 32.7 per cent undergraduate students of technical professional courses are high, moderate and low aspirant respectively, whereas 23.8 per cent, 42.7 per cent and 33.6 per cent undergraduate students of non-technical professional courses are high, moderate and low aspirant respectively. Thus, the percentage of high aspirant is higher among students of technical professional courses than the students of non-technical professional courses, whereas the percentage of moderate and low aspirant are higher in the later group than the former group.

(19) Undergraduate students of technical professional courses are significantly higher in their level of aspiration score than the undergraduate students of non-technical professional courses.

(20) 21.8 per cent, 40.1 per cent and 38.1 per cent male undergraduate students of professional courses are high, moderate and low aspirant respectively, whereas 18.8 per cent, 43 per cent and

38.3 per cent are high, moderate and low aspirant respectively in case of female undergraduate students of professional courses. Thus, the percentage of high aspirant is higher among the male students of professional courses than their female counterparts; whereas the percentage of moderate aspirant is higher in the female. In case of low aspirant the percentage is similar between the two groups.

(21) There is no significant difference in the level of aspiration score between male and female undergraduate students of professional courses, though male group is higher in the mean score of level of aspiration than the female group.

(22) 30.4 per cent, 37.7 per cent and 31.9 per cent male undergraduate students of technical professional courses are high, moderate and low aspirant respectively, whereas with regard the female undergraduate students of technical professional courses, 30 per cent, 40 per cent and 30 per cent are high, moderate and low aspirant respectively. Thus, no remarkable divergence is observed between the male and female undergraduate students of technical professional courses so far the percentage of cases with different level of aspiration is concerned.

(23) There is no significant difference in the level of aspiration score between male and female undergraduate students of technical professional courses.

(24) 23.4 per cent, 48.4 per cent and 28.1 per cent male students of non-technical professional courses are high, moderate and low aspirant respectively, whereas 27.9 per cent, 40.5 per cent and 31.7 per cent female students of non-technical professional courses are high, moderate and low aspirant respectively. Thus, percentage of high and low aspirant is higher among the female group in comparison to male group of non-technical professional courses, whereas the percentage of moderate aspirant students is higher among the later group than the former group.

(25) There is no significant difference in the level of aspiration score between male and female undergraduate students of non-technical professional courses.

(26) 30.4 per cent, 37.7 per cent and 31.9 per cent male undergraduate students of technical professional courses are high, moderate and low aspirant respectively, while 23.4 per cent, 48.4 per cent and 28.1 per cent male students of non-technical professional courses are high, moderate and low aspirant respectively.

(27) Male undergraduate students of technical professional courses are significantly higher than the male undergraduate students of non-technical professional courses in their level of aspiration score.

(28) With regard to the female undergraduate students of technical professional courses, 30 per cent, 40 per cent and 30 per cent are found high, moderate and low aspirant respectively, whereas 27.9 per cent, 40.5 per cent and 31.7 per cent are found high, moderate and low aspirant respectively.

(29) There is no significant difference in the level of aspiration score between female undergraduate students of technical and non-technical professional courses.

(30) 20.5 per cent, 41.3 per cent and 38.2 per cent undergraduate students of professional courses are high, moderate and low aspirant respectively.

(31) Both male and female undergraduate students of technical professional courses are higher in the mean scores of level of aspiration than their non-technical professional counterparts Thus, irrespective of their gender the students of technical professional courses are higher in comparison to the students of non-technical professional courses in their goal setting behaviour.

(32) Level of aspiration score is significantly correlated with theoretical and religious value dimensions, whereas it is not significantly correlated with remaining four value dimensions namely, economic, social, political and aesthetic so far as the undergraduate students of technical professional courses are concerned. On the other hand, level of aspiration score is significantly correlated with economic and religious value dimensions, whereas it has no significant correlation with

remaining four value dimensions namely, theoretical, social, political and aesthetic of undergraduate students of non-technical professional courses.

(33) Level of aspiration score is significantly correlated with three value dimensions namely, theoretical, economic and religious of both male and female undergraduate students of professional courses. On the other hand, it has no significant correlation with social, political and aesthetic value dimensions of both the groups.

(34) There is significant correlation between scores on level of aspiration and theoretical value dimension of both male and female undergraduate students of technical professional courses. On the other hand, it has no significant correlation with remaining five value dimensions namely, economic, social, political, aesthetic and religious of both male and female undergraduate students of technical professional courses.

(35) Level of aspiration score is significantly correlated with economic and religious value dimensions of male undergraduate students of non-technical professional courses, whereas it is significantly correlated with theoretical and economic value dimensions of female undergraduate students of non-technical professional courses. On the other hand, level of aspiration is not significantly correlated with theoretical, social, political and aesthetic value dimensions of male and social, political, aesthetic and religious value dimensions of female undergraduate students of non-technical professional courses.

(36) Level of aspiration score is significantly correlated with theoretical value dimension of male undergraduate students of technical professional courses, whereas it is significantly correlated with economic and religious value dimensions of male undergraduate students of non-technical professional courses.

(37) Level of aspiration score is significantly correlated with theoretical value dimension of female undergraduate students of technical professional courses, whereas it is significantly

correlated with theoretical and economic value dimensions of female undergraduate students of non-technical professional courses.

(38) Level of aspiration score is significantly correlated with theoretical, economic and religious value dimensions of undergraduate students of professional courses, while it is not significantly correlated with social, political and aesthetic value dimensions.

(39) Theoretical, economic and religious value dimensions are significantly correlated with level of aspiration score in case of almost all the target groups. The remaining three value dimensions namely, social, political and aesthetic are not significantly correlated with level of aspiration in any of the target group whether it is technical and non-technical professional group, male and female professional group, male and female technical professional group or male and female non-technical professional group.

(40) There is no significant difference in the relationship of scores on level of aspiration and each of the six value dimensions between undergraduate students of technical and non-technical professional courses.

(41) There is no significant difference in the relationship of scores on level of aspiration and each of the six value dimensions between male and female undergraduate students of professional courses.

(42) There is no significant difference in the relationship of scores on level of aspiration and each of the six value dimensions between male and female undergraduate students of technical professional courses.

(43) There is no significant difference in the relationship of scores on level of aspiration and each of the six value dimensions between male and female undergraduate students of non-technical professional courses.

(44) There is no significant difference in the relationship of scores on level of aspiration and each of the six value dimensions between male undergraduate students of technical and non-technical professional courses.

(45) There is no significant difference in the relationship of scores on level of aspiration and each of the six value dimensions between female undergraduate students of technical and non-technical professional courses.

(46) Level of aspiration is positive predictor of three value dimensions namely, theoretical, economic and social and negative predictor of remaining three value dimensions namely, political, aesthetic and religious so far the undergraduate students of technical professional courses are concerned. On the other hand, level of aspiration is positive predictor of theoretical and economic value dimensions, and negative predictor of social, political, aesthetic and religious value dimensions of students of non-technical professional courses.

(47) Level of aspiration contributes most towards religious followed by theoretical value and least towards social followed by political value of students of technical professional courses, whereas it contributes most towards economic followed by religious value and least towards aesthetic followed by social value for students of non-technical professional courses. However, the coefficient of forecasting efficiency result reveals that prediction of all the value dimensions by level of aspiration of both the groups are poorly efficient.

(48) Level of aspiration is positive predictor of theoretical and economic value dimensions of both male and female undergraduate students of professional courses, while it is negative predictor of social, political, aesthetic and religious value dimensions of both the groups.

(49) Level of aspiration contributes most towards religious followed by theoretical value and least towards social followed by aesthetic value of male undergraduate students of professional courses, whereas it contributes most towards theoretical followed by religious value and least towards political followed by social value of the female undergraduate students of professional courses. However, the coefficient of forecasting efficiency result reveals that prediction of all the value dimensions by level of aspiration of both male and female groups are poorly efficient.

(50) Level of aspiration is positive predictor of theoretical, economic and social value dimensions, and negative predictor of political, aesthetic and religious value dimensions of male undergraduate students of technical professional courses; while it is positive predictor of four value dimensions namely, theoretical, economic, social and political; and negative predictor of the remaining two value dimensions i.e. aesthetic and religious in case of female undergraduate students of technical professional courses.

(51) Level of aspiration contributes most towards by religious followed by theoretical value and least towards aesthetic followed by social value of male undergraduate students of technical professional courses, whereas it contributes most towards theoretical followed by religious value and least towards political followed by social value in case of the female students of technical professional courses. However, the coefficient of forecasting efficiency result shows that prediction of all the value dimensions by level of aspiration of both male and female students of technical professional courses are poorly efficient.

(52) Level of aspiration is positive predictor of two value dimensions of both male and female undergraduate students of non-technical professional courses. These are theoretical and economic, while negative predictor of the remaining four values namely, social, political, aesthetic and religious for both the groups.

(53) Level of aspiration contributes most towards economic value and least towards political value of both male and female students of non-technical professional courses. The coefficients of forecasting efficiency shows that level of aspiration is relatively poor predictor of all the value dimensions of both male and female undergraduate students of non-technical professional courses.

(54) Level of aspiration is positive predictor of theoretical, economic and social value dimensions, and negative predictor of political, aesthetic and religious value dimensions of male undergraduate students of technical professional courses;

while it is positive predictor of theoretical and economic value dimensions and negative predictor of social, political, aesthetic and religious value dimensions in case of male undergraduate students of non-technical professional courses.

(55) Level of aspiration contributes most towards by religious followed by theoretical value and least towards aesthetic value of male undergraduate students of technical professional courses, whereas it contributes most towards economic followed by religious value and least towards political value in case of male undergraduate students of non-technical professional courses.

(56) Level of aspiration is positive predictor of four value dimensions namely, theoretical, economic, social and political; and negative predictor of aesthetic and religious value dimensions of the female undergraduate students of technical professional courses. On the other hand, level of aspiration is positive predictor of theoretical and economic value dimensions; and negative predictor of remaining four value dimensions namely, social, political, aesthetic and religious in case of female undergraduate students of non-technical professional courses.

(57) Level of aspiration contributes most towards theoretical followed by religious value and least towards political followed by social value of the female students of technical professional courses, whereas it contributes most towards economic followed by theoretical value and least towards political followed by social value of female students of non-technical professional courses.

(58) Level of aspiration is positive predictor of theoretical and economic value dimensions, and negative predictor of the remaining four value dimensions namely, social, political, aesthetic and religious of undergraduate students of professional courses. The contribution of level of aspiration towards prediction of value dimensions is highest towards religious value (negatively) followed by theoretical value (positively), whereas lowest towards social followed by political value (both negatively). However, the coefficient of

forecasting efficiency result reveals that predictions of all the value dimensions are poorly efficient.

(59) Though order changed, theoretical, religious and economic value dimensions are most contributed by level of aspiration in all the cases. Religious and theoretical values remain prominent in both male and female of technical professional group, whereas economic, religious and theoretical values remain prominent in case of non-technical professional group of which economic and religious values for males and economic and theoretical values for females.

(60) Though, more or less, level of aspiration contributes in the prediction of all the six value dimensions of all groups of samples, the forecasting efficiency coefficient of no regression equation is found to exceed 6.78 per cent, which is recorded for the regression equation of level of aspiration on economic value dimension of male students of non-technical professional courses.

5.2. Educational Implications and Suggestions

The findings of the present study have raised some of the issues that are to be addressed with great care and dedication for creating a value-based human society. Based on the findings, the following recommendations are made to revive, develop and foster culturally desirable human values among undergraduate students.

(1) The present study has revealed that undergraduate students of professional courses give higher importance on theoretical and economic values, while they give lower importance on aesthetic and religious values. Religion has always occupied a central place in human society. It is the supremely integrating and unifying force in human society, when practised in right way. It is religion that directs human beings to renounce unsocial activities and enables a person to control his/her wants and desires. Love and service to others are two great teachings of religion. It is much pitiful that such eternal values are given lowest preference by students of higher education. Similarly, they placed lower importance to aesthetic

value, which implies that form, symmetry, artistic pursuits etc. have become meaningless for the undergraduate students of professional courses today. These highest values are replaced by sense of material wealth, practicability, power etc., because the study shows that they give higher importance on economic value. Inclining more towards knowledge and material wealth without any care for great religious and aesthetic virtues is a catastrophe for social balance and cohesion. Therefore, conscious and deliberate efforts need to be undertaken by the teachers, educational administrators, and policy-makers so as to integrate the curricular and co-curricular activities with sound religious teachings and aesthetic virtues. But, at the same time, much care should be taken to keep religion away from fundamentalism, conservatism and everything else which can make our students communal and religious bigots.

(2) Similarly, the social value is given relatively lower rank i.e. fourth position by all the target groups irrespective of nature/type of course and gender. This implies that irrespective of nature/type of course and gender, the undergraduate students of professional courses give relatively less importance to values which are concerning to society like brotherhood, courtesy, forgiveness, freedom, friendship, gratitude, hospitality, justice, love, patience, service, sympathy, team spirit, tolerance, accountability, dutifulness, concern for environment etc. This is a very awful situation for the human society. Therefore, higher education institutions in general and institutions of professional courses in particular should take cognizance to incorporate different co-curricular activities such as music, art, drama, community service, NCC, NSS, Scouts and Guides, Red Cross, field Strips, visits to hospitals and orphan villages, organising talks on great social leaders, observing festivals of different socio-religions groups, sports and games etc. in a balanced way so that social values can be properly transmitted.

(3) Several institutions of professional courses are imparting value-based education to protect human values. Some institutions and universities of professional courses in India

have included some subjects related to value orientation as 'Business Ethics', 'Management of Values', or 'Indian Ethos of Management' and so on. But, it is necessary that teaching of essential human values in professional courses should be done in a more organised way. A course exclusively on value education may not be absolute necessity for the purpose. Value education can effectively be imparted through making necessary adjustment in the regular curricular and co-curricular activities even in professional courses. In commerce subjects topics like Dignity of Labour; Professional Ethics; Corruption, Exploitation and their impact on social order; Significance of cultural heritage in economy of India etc. can be incorporated. Similarly, for science subjects topics like History of great scientists, ethics and qualities they possessed; Relationship between science, religion and spirituality; Use of Science for improving life-style and removing evils from society like poverty, unemployment, corruption, exploitation etc. can be included. However, the teachers are to play the most prominent role in this respect as they are the person who transmits the curriculum to the students. They are to develop themselves into inspiring personalities and cherish values in their own life. They are to be dedicated, responsible and accountable towards the profession. Necessary training should also be given to teachers so that they can directly shoulder the responsibility to inculcate right values among students. Moreover, the management of institutions should be made very firm, clear and student friendly. Thus, all the aspects of education like students, teachers, curriculum and administration should work in a collaborative mode to develop eternal and supreme values among students.

(4) Results have shown that students of professional courses endorse diverse level of aspiration. Moreover, level of aspiration is found significantly correlated with theoretical, economic and religious value dimensions of undergraduate students of professional courses. Therefore, guidance and counselling cell should mandatorily be established in every institutions of higher education to facilitate the students to set

their level of aspiration in perfect consonance with their own psycho-physical potentialities, abilities and socio-economic background. Counselling service should be regularly conducted to enable the students to develop righteousness in their thought, speech and action.

(5) Besides the concerns of formal education, parents should also be conscious for developing good moral habits among their offspring's right from the early stages. They should exhibit desirable qualities in their own behaviour and try to become role model for their children. Freedom may be allowed but should be accompanied with some sort of restraints. A congenial rearing up practice and home environment can go a long way in fostering right values among individuals.

5.3. Suggestions for Further Research

(1) A similar study may be undertaken in other states and results may be compared with the present one.

(2) The present study is undertaken only on undergraduate students of professional courses. A comparative study with the same variables may be conducted between the undergraduate students of professional and non-professional courses, which will provide a comprehensive idea regarding the influence of education system in value formation.

(3) The present study may be replicated among secondary school students as well as postgraduate students, in order to understand the nature of value formation throughout different stages of development.

(4) As the present study reveals that level of aspiration is a poor predictor of value dimensions, therefore, studies may be conducted to find out other socio-psychological factors that might influence value dimensions of undergraduate students of professional courses like wishes, interests, intelligence, self-concept, personality traits, past experiences, racial background, religion, rearing up practice, parental attitude, home environment, socio-economic status, social expectations, peer influence, education, teachers' attitude and values, institutional climate, culture, media etc.

(5) Comparative studies on value dimensions as well as level of aspiration may be undertaken among students belonging to different social classes and castes like ST, SC, OBC, General, Minority, Rich and Poor class, Literate and Illiterate, Rural and Urban etc.

(6) Comparative studies with same variables between students studying in public and private institutions at secondary as well as degree level will be a fruitful area for further research.

(7) The present study may be replicated taking the physically challenged students as target population.

5.4. Conclusion

Values form an integral part of human personality and act as guiding principles of life which influence our thought, speech and action in conscious and unconscious manner. They provide the platform for decision-making process and determine our final course of action among alternative choices. Desirable values are like the oil that helps to keep the machine of society running smoothly. It is, therefore, very essential that education should develop such values among the students that they become individuals of sterling character who place service of the society above the service of the self.

The findings referred in the present study have clearly indicated that the nature of value formation is a complex and multidimensional process. The present study examines the influence of level of aspiration in the process of value formation, where inadequate findings are documented. Though, it is found that some of the value dimensions are significantly influenced by level of aspiration, yet this may not be sufficient evidence to understand the process of value formation. There might have some other factors apart from level of aspiration which might influence the process of value formation like home environment, area of residence, rearing up practice, parents' aspiration and expectations, socio-economic status, psycho-physical traits, academic traits, self-concept, risk-taking behaviour, achievement motivation, peer-influences etc. that should receive attention of researchers in the near future.

The result of the present study has confirmed our general assumption that the present society gives more importance to materialism rather than highest virtues like humanism, socialism and spiritualism. The study has revealed that irrespective of gender and nature of education, the undergraduate students of professional courses give more weightage to economic value in comparison to social, aesthetic and religious value dimensions. It is pitiful that all the groups of students under consideration in the study give relatively lower i.e. fourth preference to social value out of six. Of course, it is not their fault to do so. They are being nurtured in a dreadful environment which is dominated by material greed. There was a time when we used to teach students to satisfy with limited needs. But today we teach *"Sky is the Limit'*. Consciously or unconsciously, we let them not to limit the success with a definite end. Rather to grow higher and higher and the way is ready for that i.e. nothing but science and technology. There was a time when it was thought that for observing morality, religious practice is necessary. But, today the concept has changed. The modern philosophy influenced mostly by western thought advocates that in order to observe morality and humanity, religion is not required. Such kind of one-sided importance is somehow responsible for lower interest of present day adolescents towards socialistic attitude, form and harmony etc. as evident in the present study. In recent times, we are more striving towards modernisation with emphasis on science and technology, which has made us to abandoned many traditional values and belief systems. The values, attitudes and beliefs which are important for maintaining social cohesion and solidarity has completely vanished. Technological or attitudinal whatever may be the reason, no one can deny the fact that the present value crisis is creating serious threats to individuals, society, the nation and the globe at large. Education has also failed in its very purpose of creating a value-based society.

The Indian culture is deeply rooted in spiritual values and unless these values find their way into the life of students, education will lose its significance. It is the students of today who are to be in charge of the various departments of life tomorrow; and if they learn what real integrity in their early years, they are not likely to step up in the wrong path in future. Every effort must, therefore, be made to teach students true values from the very earlier stage of their educational life.

Of course, professional education which inclines students towards materialism is becoming more vital in recent times. This happens because of specified labour market which demands more skilled persons in different professions. Moreover, in a country like India where unemployment rate is almost 10 per cent, career oriented professional education is of utmost significance. But, at the same time such career oriented professional education must take initiative to instruct the students the desirable human values. Considering to the deplorable condition, there is an urgent need to adopt such means and methods which are effective in promoting human values by making necessary arrangement in curricular and co-curricular activities. Of course, awareness at all levels is growing to revive and reform the values of human life and to rejuvenate the foundation of human civilisation through introducing an exclusive subject on value education. But, unless and until values cover the whole array of curricular and co-curricular activities such effort may not prove much successful. In fact all programmes, all activities of educational institutions should reflect desirable values. Next to the delineation of the curricular and co-curricular activities, the teachers hold the supreme responsibility. Teachers should necessarily be trained in the know-how to adopt and modify their instructions with appropriate strategies to inculcate values among students. Responsibility of educational administrators, students, parents and elder members of the society is not less important in this regard. An exemplary behaviour of elders and a congenial and conducive environment both at home and schools can go a long way in the acquisition of right values. So it is high time that parents, teachers and all segments of populations should work with sincere dedication and faith to accomplish what Education Commission 1964-66 believed, "........... *India should strive to bring science and values of the spirit together in harmony and thereby pave their way for the eventual emergence of a society which would cater to the needs of the whole man and not a particular fragment of his personality*" (Aggarwal, J.C., 2010)

India is on the move today with the promise of new renaissance in the making. The most powerful tool in the process of this renaissance and modernisation is value-based education in one hand and science and technology on the other hand. Why are we in dilemma to choose one? Why can't we combine the progress of science and technology along with progress of mind and spirit also? In this context we cannot do better than to quote Pt. Jawaharlal Nehru, "................*We cannot be untrue to science because that represents the basic fact of life today. Still less can we be untrue to those essential principles for which India has stood in the past throughout the ages. Let us then pursue our path to industrial progress with our strength and vigour and at the same time remember that material riches without toleration and compassion and wisdom may well turn to dust and ashes.*" (Aggarwal, J.C., 2010)

5.5. Summary of the Study

Background

Value literally means something that has a price, something precious and worthwhile. This may be material or concrete aspects as well as non-material or abstract concepts like state of mind, interests, truthfulness, peace, happiness etc. Different philosophies, theories and views associated with values- Eastern as well as Western come to a point of consensus that values are the normative ethics which guide us to decide what is right, good, desirable, ought to be and vice-versa and serve as the grounds for our decision-making process and the final course of action that is acceptable by the society and culture to which we belong. Values motivate, define and colour all our activities- Cognitive, Affective and Psycho-motor. Thus, a vibrant set of values provide the basis for principles of life that give direction and firmness to life and bring joy, satisfaction, peace and quality to life in the same way as the rail keep a train on the track and help it move smoothly and quickly with direction without any accident.

But, unfortunately in the modern times, the valuing of men has shifted from spiritualism to materialism, from humanism to barbarism. The material pursuit has become the be-all and end-all of life. With the advancement of science and technology in the twenty-first century the civilisation has conquered the moon but simultaneously the barbaric and valueless tendencies like selfishness, clashes, corruption, nepotism, hypocrisy, violence, immorality, terrorism, crime, murder, rape, agitation, self-centred egoism, youth unrest, eve-teasing, exploitation etc. are dominating our lives. Human virtues like love, sympathy, honesty, purity of mind, selflessness, wisdom, mercy, humility, faithfulness, obedience, sincerity etc. remain only the words of dictionary.

India is a country with diversified culture which was rich in its traditional beliefs and value systems. It is the land which is known to the whole world as the custodian of the 'soul', is becoming the land without soul now. The Ancient Indian system of education entirely concentrated on moral and spiritual development of minds. The whole of Vedic education and even the Post-Vedic lectures like the Ramayana, the Mahabharata, the Geeta etc. are the treasure house of values. The holy Quran also stresses the importance of human values. The importance of value education has also been duly recognised by different committees and commissions on education appointed in India so far. The Hartog Committee (1929), the Central Advisory Broad of Education in 1946, Secondary Education Commission (1953), the Sri Prakasa Committee, Kothari Commission (1964-66), National Policy on Education (1986) etc. all have emphasised the direct or indirect instruction of social, moral, and religious values in educational institutions. But in spite of the steady efforts, value education is being neglected to a great extent. The majority of educational institutions have failed in evolving an integrated approach in the curricular and co-curricular programmes for the all round development of human personality. Our present educational system with all its complexities and intricacies, have proved to be deficient so far, as it neglects or does not give deserving importance to values in human life (Venkataiah, N., 1998). The prime objective of education today is no longer the formation of character and promotion of values, but the emphasis is on promotion of technical knowhow, skills, and technologies for material progress.

Underlying much of the research studies, it is implicit that value dimensions are essentially related, influenced and shaped by factors like sex, type of education received, home environment, intelligence and some other socio-economic and psychological factor. So far the value dimensions of undergraduate students are concerned, it is evident from the review of related literature made that most of the studies conducted so far are on the students of conventional courses viz. arts, science and commerce, whereas it is not adequately investigated targeting the students of professional courses. Only a few studies are found which aimed at identification of values of students of either business studies or medical course or teacher education etc. Except, Manav, Ram Niwas (1981), who conducted his study on attitudes, self-concept and values of professional and non-professional college students, no other study is reported so far to reveal the value dimensions of undergraduate students of professional courses at large. A similar picture is revealed with regard to relationship between level of aspiration and value dimensions also. Only three studies by Macneil (1990), Basolene (1992), and Ranu, Sarbjit Kaur (1995) are found in this regard. Further analysis showed that none of these three studies aimed at investigating the relationship between the two variables targeting the undergraduate students of professional courses involving a comparison between students of technical and non-technical professional courses. Considering the paucity of research in this area the need of the present work is justified.

Objectives

(ix) To study the value preferences of undergraduate students of both technical and non-technical professional courses of Gauhati University.

(x) To examine whether there is significant difference between undergraduate students of technical and non-technical professional courses in their value dimensions.

(xi) To study the level of aspiration of undergraduate students of both technical and non-technical professional courses of Gauhati University.

(xii) To determine the relationship between value dimensions and level of aspiration of undergraduate students of technical and non-technical professional courses.

(xiii) To determine the relationship between value dimensions and level of aspiration of male and female undergraduate students of professional courses.

(xiv) To examine whether there is significant difference in the relationship of value dimensions and level of aspiration between undergraduate students of technical and non-technical professional courses.

(xv) To examine whether there is significant difference in the relationship of value dimensions and level of aspiration between male and female undergraduate students of professional courses.

(xvi) To study the level of aspiration as predictor of value dimensions of undergraduate students of both technical and non-technical professional courses.

Hypotheses

The following hypotheses are formulated in order to meet the objectives.

Ho_1: There is no significant difference between undergraduate students of technical and non-technical professional courses in their value dimensions.

Ho_2: There is no significant difference between undergraduate students of technical and non-technical professional courses in their level of aspiration score.

Ho_3: There is no significant relationship between value dimensions and level of aspiration of undergraduate students of technical and non-technical professional courses.

Ho_4: There is no significant relationship between value dimensions and level of aspiration of male and female undergraduate students of professional courses.

Ho_5: There is no significant difference in the relationship of value dimensions and level of aspiration between undergraduate students of technical and non-technical professional courses.

Ho_6: There is no significant difference in the relationship of value dimensions and level of aspiration between male and female undergraduate students of professional courses.

Ho_7: Level of aspiration is the predictor of value dimensions of undergraduate students of both technical and non-technical professional courses.

Methodology

The present study has been conducted under the descriptive method. In fact, it is a descriptive correlational research. Descriptive correlational studies are those studies which try to test the hypotheses on relationship between two or more variables. Therefore, this method is considered to be the most appropriate in the present investigation as it aimed at a study of value dimensions of students and to reveal its relationship with level of aspiration.

Identification of Population

The present study has aimed at a study of the six value dimensions namely, theoretical, economic, aesthetic, social, political and religious as classified by Edward Sprenger (1928), of undergraduate students of professional courses and their relationship with level of aspiration. The study also involves a comparison on these two variables i.e. *Value Dimensions* and *Level of Aspiration* between the students of technical and non-technical professional courses. It is delimited to the undergraduate degree colleges of professional courses affiliated to Gauhati University which are 83 in count by the end of 2012, of which 16 are colleges of technical professional courses and 67 are colleges of non-technical professional courses. The study excludes those conventional degree colleges which offer one or two professional subjects. As such, the study has included all the students irrespective of sex and locality enrolled at undergraduate level in all the 83 degree colleges affiliated to Gauhati University offering education in professional courses during the study period of 2010 to 2013 as its population.

Sampling Design

In the present study sampling has been done at two levels as (A) Selection of sample colleges and (B) Selection of sample students.

(A) Selection of Sample Colleges

Stratified Random Sampling method has been employed in selecting the sample colleges. As the study involves a comparison between undergraduate students of technical and non-technical professional courses, hence the colleges of professional courses affiliated to Gauhati University are first divided into two homogenous 'strata' as 'colleges of technical professional courses' and 'colleges of non-technical professional courses' which are 16 and 67 in number respectively. Thereafter, 30% of the colleges are randomly selected from both the stratums as sample colleges for the present study. Thus, a total of 25 undergraduate degree colleges of professional courses (05 colleges of technical professional courses and 20 colleges of non-technical professional courses) are taken as sample for the present study.

(B) Selection of Sample Students

Since the study includes 'Gender' as one of the variables for analysis, stratified random sampling method has been employed for selection of sample students from each of the selected colleges to ensure a representative and cross-section of the population (male and female) in the samples. There are altogether 4143 students in five selected colleges of technical professional courses of which 2747 are male and 1396 are female. Similarly, there are 2850 students in 20 selected colleges of non-technical professional courses of which 1272 are male and 1568 are female. Applying proportionate allocation, 5 per cent of students from both stratums 'Male' and 'Female' has been taken from each of the colleges separately to guarantee a more representative distribution of students throughout the colleges. Thus, the total sample for the present study consists of 351 undergraduate students of professional courses of which 208 are students of technical professional courses (138 male and 70 female) and 143 are students of non-technical professional courses (64 male and 79 female).

Tools of Data Collection

The following standardised tools have been employed considering the objectives of the study and feasibility of their use.

Sl No.	*Name of the Tool*	*Variables Investigated*	*Contents of the Tool*	*Developed by*
1.	STUDY OF VALUES TEST (SVT)	Value Dimensions	Theoretical, Economic, Aesthetic, Social, Political and Religious	Dr. R. K. Ojha and Dr. Mahesh Bhargava
2.	LEVEL OF ASPIRATION MEASURE (LOA)	Level of Aspiration	Goal Discrepancy, Attainment Discrepancy and Number of Times Goal Reached	Dr. Mahesh Bhargava and Late Prof. M.A. Shah

Treatment of Data

The data that have been gathered for the present study is of quantitative type. Hence, only quantitative approach of treating data has been used in the present context. As the present study is mainly based on examining group performances and relationship between variables, the statistical techniques employed for the study are 'Frequency', 'Percentage', 'Mean', 'sd', 't-test', 'Correlation', 'Linear regression' and 'Coefficients of Forecasting Efficiency'. five pre cent level of statistical significance is considered in the whole analysis. *'Statistical Package for Social Sciences (SPSS)'* software has been used in analysing the row data.

Major Findings

In order to have a bird's eye view of the findings of the study, the analysis and discussions are made in the order of the objectives of the study. On the basis of the analysis, the following major findings are arrived at.

1. The preference order of value dimensions of undergraduate students of technical professional courses is theoretical, followed by economic, political, social, aesthetic and religious which is economic followed by theoretical, political, social, aesthetic and religious for students of non-technical professional courses. Thus, except the two most preferred value dimensions, the preference order of remaining four value dimensions is same between the two groups.
2. There is significant difference between undergraduate students of technical and non-technical professional courses with respect to three value dimensions namely, theoretical, economic and social. The students of technical professional courses scored significantly higher than their non-technical counterparts in theoretical and economic values, while the later group scored significantly higher than the former group in social value. No significant difference is found between the two groups with respect to the remaining three value dimensions namely, political, aesthetic and religious.

3. 28.9 per cent, 38.5 per cent and 32.7 per cent undergraduate students of technical professional courses are high, moderate and low aspirant respectively, whereas 23.8 per cent, 42.7 per cent and 33.6 per cent undergraduate students of non-technical professional courses are high, moderate and low aspirant respectively.
4. Undergraduate students of technical professional courses are significantly higher in their level of aspiration score than the undergraduate students of non-technical professional courses.
5. Level of aspiration score is significantly correlated with theoretical and religious value dimensions, whereas it is not significantly correlated with remaining four value dimensions namely, economic, social, political and aesthetic so far the undergraduate students of technical professional courses are concerned. On the other hand, level of aspiration is significantly correlated with economic and religious value dimensions, whereas it has no significant correlation with remaining four value dimensions namely, theoretical, social, political and aesthetic of undergraduate students of non-technical professional courses.
6. Level of aspiration is significantly correlated with theoretical, economic and religious value dimensions of both male and female undergraduate students of professional courses. On the other hand, it has no significant correlation with social, political and aesthetic value dimensions of both the groups.
7. There is no significant difference in the relationship of scores on level of aspiration and each of the six value dimensions between undergraduate students of technical and non-technical professional courses.
8. There is no significant difference in the relationship of scores on level of aspiration and each of the six value dimensions between male and female undergraduate students of professional courses.
9. Level of aspiration is positive predictor of theoretical, economic and social value dimensions and negative predictor of political, aesthetic and religious value dimensions of

undergraduate students of technical professional courses. On the other hand, level of aspiration is positive predictor of theoretical and economic value dimensions, and negative predictor of social, political, aesthetic and religious value dimensions of undergraduate students of non-technical professional courses.

10. Level of aspiration contributes most towards religious followed by theoretical value and least towards social followed by political value of undergraduate students of technical professional courses. On the other hand, level of aspiration contributes most towards economic followed by religious value and least towards aesthetic followed by social value for students of non-technical professional courses. However, the coefficients of forecasting efficiency result reveals that prediction of all the value dimensions by level of aspiration of both the groups are poorly efficient.

Conclusion

The present study has revealed that undergraduate students of professional courses give higher importance on theoretical and economic values, while they give lower importance on aesthetic and religious values. Moreover, all the groups of students irrespective of their gender and course of study give relatively lower i.e. fourth preference to social value out of six. Thus, the result of the present study has confirmed our general assumption that the present generation gives more importance to materialism rather than highest virtues like humanism, socialism, spiritualism, form and harmony etc. Of course, there are reasons behind such awful situations. Today, the students are being nurtured in a dreadful environment which is dominated by material greed. There was a time when we used to teach students to satisfy with limited needs. But today we say *"Sky is the Limit'* and teach them to soar high in the sky with the help of science and technology. Technological or attitudinal-whatever may be the reason of present value crisis situation, there is an urgent need to adopt such means and methods which are effective in promoting human values. And the best way in this direction is none but value based education in general and higher education in particular.

The findings referred in the present study further indicated that the nature of value formation is a complex and multidimensional process. Though, it is found that some of value dimensions are significantly influenced by level of aspiration, yet this may not be sufficient evidence to understand the process of value formation. There might have some other factors apart from level of aspiration which might influence the process of value formation that should receive attention of researchers in the near future.

Bibliography

- Abu-Hilal, M. M. (2000). A Structural model of Attitude towards School Subjects, Academic Aspiration and Achievement. *Educational Psychology*, *20*(1), 75-84.
- Agarwal, J. C. (2010). *Education for Values, Environment and Human Rights.* Shipra Publications, Delhi-110002.
- Arceneaux, Cathann (1990). *Personality characteristics, interests and values of differentially achieving able college students* (Ph. D. Thesis). Iowa University. In *Dissertation Abstracts International*, *52*(3), 830-A.
- Association of Indian Universities (2000). *Value Education in India.* Selections from University News-7, AIU, New Delhi.
- Backer and Seigal (1957). Reference Groups, Membership Groups and Attitude Change. *Journal of Abnormal Social Psychology*, *55*, 360-364.
- Bahm, A. J. (1982). Value Oriented Education (Part-III). *The Progress of Education*, August,1982.
- Bahm, A. J. (1982). Value Oriented Education (Part-IV). *The Progress of Education*, September,1982.
- Bandura, A., Barbaranelli, C., Caprara, G. V., and Pastorelli, C. (2001). Self-efficacy beliefs as shapers of children's aspirations and career trajectories, *Child Development, 72*, 187-206.
- Basolene, Kamate Mastaki (1992). Aspirations and Values of African and Asian Theological Students: A Case Study in the United States of America. *Dissertation Abstracts International*, *53*(7), 2807.
- Bauni, Kuotsu (1992). *A Study of Values of College Students in Nagaland in relation to their Self Concept* (Unpublished Ph. D. Thesis). NEHU, Shillong, Meghalaya.

- Benjamin, B. Maxwell (2011). *Influence of Organisational Climate on the Prevalence of Moral Values among the Higher Secondary Students in Chennai City* (Unpublished Ph. D. Thesis). Bharathidasan University, Tiruchirappalli, Tamil Nadu, India.
- Best, J. W. and Kahn, J. V. (2008). *Research in Education,* Prentice Hall of India Private Limited, New Delhi.
- Bhagawati, Binita (1999). *Comparative Analysis of Value Orientation of Two School Systems* (Unpublished Ph. D. Thesis). Gauhati University, Assam.
- Bhandari, M. S. (2000). Value Education, Secularism and Religion; *Value Education in India, Selections from University News-7.* Association of Indian Universities, New Delhi.
- Bharadwaj, T. R. (2001). *Education of Human Values.* Mittal Publications, New Delhi.
- Bhargava, M., and Shah, M. A. *Mannual for Level of Aspiration Measure (LOA).* National Psychological Corporation, Agra-04.
- Bhatia, K., and Bhatia, B. D. (1977). *The Philosophical and Sociological Foundations of Education.* Doaba House Book Sellers New Delhi.
- Bhatia, K., and Bhatia, B. D. (1986). *Theory and Principles of Education.* (1seventh Ed.). Seena Offset Press, New Delhi.
- Bhatt, P. D. (2005). *A Comparative Study of Level of Aspiration, Self-Confidence, Risk-taking Tendency and Will to Win among Male and Female Sports Persons* (Unpublished Ph. D. Thesis). Kumaun University, Nainital.
- Bobowi, Magdalena (2011). What is the Better Predictor of Students' Personal Values: Parents' values or Students' Personality? *International Journal of Intercultural Relations, 35*(4),488-498.
- Bond, R., and Saunders, P. (1999). Routes of Success: Influences on the occupational attainment of young British males. *British Journal of Sociology, 50*, 217–249.
- Boxer, P., and others (2011). Educational Aspiration-Expectation Discrepancies: Relation to Socio-Economic Status and Academic Risk-Related Factors. *Journal of Adolescence, 34*(4), 609-617.

- Boyd, G. F. (1952). The Levels of Aspiration of White and Negro Children in a Non-Segregated Elementary Schools. *Journal of Social Psychology, 36,* 191-196.
- Brubacher, J. S. (1962). *Modern Philosophies of Education.* McGrow Hill Book Co., New York.
- Buch, M. B. *(1988). Fourth Survey of Research in Education.* NCERT, New Delhi.
- Chakraborty, S. K. *(1991). Managament of Values: Towards Cultural Congruence.* Oxford University Press.
- Chakraborty, S. K. (1999). *Values and Ethics for Organisations : Theory and practice.* Oxford University Press, New Delhi.
- Chauhan, V. L., and Kothari, P. (1997). Personal Values: A Motivator for Women's Empowerment. *Indian Psychological Abstracts and Reviews, 4*(1), 150.
- Chilana, M. R., and Dewan, M. L. (1998). *The Human Values a Task for All.* Concept Publishing, New Delhi.
- Chittibabu, S. V. (2000). Value Orientation of Education. *Value Education in India, Selections from University News-7.* Association of Indian Universities, New Delhi.
- Christensen, K. E. (1992). Values in Administrative Decision making. *Dissertation Abstracts International, 52*(11), 3777-A.
- Chuttaura, P. (1992). *A Study of Adjustment, Aspiration and Values of scheduled caste and scheduled tribe Pupil-Teachers studying in Teachers' Training Colleges of Rajasthan* (Unpublished Ph. D. Thesis). Rajasthan University, Jaipur.
- Cochran, Daria B. (2011). Adolescent occupational Aspirations: Test of Gottfredson's Theory of Circumscription and Compromise, *Career Development Quarterly*, *59*(5), 412-427.
- Cyril, Simmons (1999). A Comparative Study of Educational and Cultural Determinants of Adolescent Values, *Journal of Beliefs & Values: Studies in Religion & Education*, *20*(2) 208-218. Retrieved from http://www.tandfonline.com/doi/abs/10.1080/1361767990200206#preview
- Dagar, B. S., and Dhull, I. (1997). A Case for Value-oriented Education. *University News, 35*(29), 10-11.

- Dash, B. N. (2004). *Trends and Issues in Indian Education.* Sterling Publishers Pvt Ltd., New Delhi.
- Dash, B. N. (2004). *Principles of Education and Education in the Emerging Indian Society.* Ajanta Prakashan, Delhi-06.
- Dembo, T. (1931). Der Arger Als Dynamisches Problem Untersuchungen Eur Mandlungsund Affekt Psychologie, X Edition by Kurt Lewin. *Psychological Forsch*, *15* (1), 144.
- Devi, B. (2000). The Degradation of Moral values among the youth in Manipur. *ECHO: A quarterly publication of Manipur University Students' Union, 9*(4), 23-24.
- Dhekwar, T. M. (1996). *A Comparative Study of Some differentiating Personality Variables and Value of Higher Secondary Students of Vocational-Technical Course in Vidarbha* (Ph.D. Thesis). Nagpur University. In *Indian Educational Abstracts, 1*(1).
- Dixit, Prabha (1998). Value Oriented Educaion in 2000 AD- A Challange. *Value Education*, APH Publishing Corporation, New Delhi.
- Domene, Jose. F. (2011). Academic Motivation in Post-secondary Students: Effects of Career Outcome Expectations and Type of Aspiration. *Canadian Journal of Education*, *34*(1), 99-127.
- Duane, H. Bajema, and others (2002), Aspirations of Rural Youth. *Journal of Agricultural Education*, *43*(3), 61-71.
- Fartiyal, Pushpalata (2005). *Study of Home Environment, Level of Aspiration and Self-Confidence as Predictors of Achievement Motivation among Professional and Non-professional College Students* (Unpublished Ph. D. Thesis). Kumaun University, Nainital.
- Ferran, C., Cristina, F., Mònica, G., and Sara, M. (2007). The Values Adolescents Aspire to, Their Well being and the Values Parents Aspire to for their Children. *Social Indicator Research, July 2007*, 271-290. Retrived from www. springerlink.metapress.com
- Fraenkel, I. R. (1977). *How to Teach about Values.* Eaglewood Cliffs, NJ: Prentice Hall.

- Frand, J. D. (1935). Individual Differences in Certain Aspects of Level of Aspiration. *Amer. Journal of Psychology, 1935(47)*, 119-128.
- Garret, H. E. (1961). *Statistics in Psycholgy and Education.* Allied Pacific Private Limited, Bombay.
- Gerdien D, BertramTroost, Simone A. de Roos and Siebren, Miedema (2009). The Relationship between Religious Education and Religious Commitments and Explorations of Adolescents on Religious Identity Development in Dutch Christian Secondary schools. *Journal of Beliefs & Values: Studies in Religion & Education, 30*(1), 17-27. Retrieved from http://www.tandfonline.com/doi/full/10.1080/13617670902784519
- Gholamreza, Sham (2004). Values in Management Education. *Edutracks*, Neelkamal Publication Pvt. Ltd., Hyderabad.
- Gomathi, P. (2008). Leadership Effectiveness and Knowledge Value of Professionals, *Journal of Community Guidance and Research.*
- Goswami, Dulumoni (2011). *Higher Education in India—Growth, Expansion and Issues.* DVS Publishers, Guwahati-01.
- Government of India. (1951). *Report of the University Education Commission, 1948-49.* GOI, New Delhi.
- Government of India. (1959). *Report of the Committee on Religious and Moral Instruction, 1959.* GOI, New Delhi.
- Government of India. (1966). *Report of the Education Commission, 1964-66.* GOI, New Delhi.
- Government of India. (1986). *Report of National Policy on Education, 1986.* GOI, New Delhi.
- Government of India. (1990). Towards an Enlightened and Human Society. *Report of the Committee of Review of National Policy on Education, 1986.* GOI, New Delhi.
- Goyal, B. R. (1998). *Values and Education in the Emerging Indian Society, Value Education.* APH Publishing Corporation, New Delhi.
- Gupta, N. L. (1999). *Neo-humanism and Human Values.* Mohit Publications, New Delhi.

- Gupta, S., and Mandal, J. M. (1997). Effects of Education, Location, Sex and Marital status on Values of an Individual. *Indian Psychological Abstracts and Reviews, 4*(1), 78.
- Gurnani, L., Bala, M., and Golwalkar, S. (1995). A study of Life Values, Personality and Creativity of Physically Hadicapped persons. *Educational Herald, 26*(1), 5-9.
- Gutman, Leslie Morrison and Akerman, Rodie (2008). Determinants of Aspirations. *Centre for Research on the Wider Benefits of Learning, Institute of Education*, 20 Bedford Way, London WC1H 0AL. Retrieved from www.learningbenefits.net
- Harbison, Joan Roberts (1991). Value Orientations and Career Aspirations of those Pursuing as MSW degree: Does the BSW make a Difference? *Dissertation Abstracts International*, *53*(2), 621.
- Hoppe, F. (1930). Erfolg and Misserfold (Unterguchungen Zur Handlongs- Und. Affect Psychologie: IX edition by Kurt Lewin). *Psychological Forsch*, *14*(1), 1-62.
- Hurlock, E. B. (1967). *Adolescent Development.* McGrow Hill Co. Inc., New York.
- Iglesias, M. E. L. and V., Ricardo B. de B. (2011). Personal and Interpersonal Value system, Self-perception and Identity of Spanish nurses: A cross-sectional study. *Journal of Beliefs & Values: Studies in Religion & Education, 32*(3), 281-294. Retrieved from http://dx.doi.org/10.1080/13617672.2011.627675)
- Islam, Sirajul (2002). *A Study of Value Pattern of College Students in relation to some select Socio-Educational Variable* (Unpublished Ph. D. Thesis). Gauhati University, Guwahati-14.
- Ismael, Abu-Saad (2003). The Work Values of Arab Teachers in Israel in a Multicultural Context. *Journal of Beliefs & Values: Studies in Religion & Education, 24*(1), 39-51. Retrieved from http://www.tandfonline.com/doi/abs/10.1080/1361767032000052980#preview
- Jafri, Bilkis Sultana (1992). *Values and Aspirations of undergraduate Women Students in Aligarh: A comparative study of Tika Ram College and A.M.U.* (Unpublished Ph. D. Thesis). Aligarh Muslim University, Aligarh.

- Jangaiah, C. (1998). Value Classification. *Value Education.* APH Publishing Corporation, New Delhi.
- Joshi, Kireet (1999). Fundamental Duties and Human Values. *The Indian Journal for Teacher Education, 2*(1), 1-5.
- Joshi, T. Chandra (2003). *A Study of Social Attitude, Level of Aspiration and Scholastic Achievement as Correlates of Self-Confidence* (Unpublished Ph. D. Thesis). Kumaun University, Nainital.
- Julia, Ipgrave (2012). Relationships between Local Patterns of Religious Practice and young people's Attitudes to the Religiosity of their peers. *Journal of Beliefs & Values: Studies in Religion & Education, 33*(3). Retrieved from http://www.tandfonline.com/doi/full/10.1080/13617672.2012.732805
- Kapur, J. N. (2000). Values in Indian Society. *Value Education in India, Selections from University News-7.* Association of Indian Universities, New Delhi.
- Kaur, Amarjeet (1993). *Value Dimensions of +2 Government and Private Secondary School Students in relation to their Sex and Parental Income* (Unpublished M. Phil. Dissertation). Punjabi University, Patiala.
- Kaur, Amarpreet (1993). *Value Dimensions of Science and Arts Post-Graduate Students in relation to their Sex and Academic Achievement* (Unpublished M. Phil. Dissertation). Punjabi University, Patiala.
- Kauts, D. S., and Kaur, G. (2010). A Study of Value Preferences among Adolescents with high and low level of Stress. *New Frontiers in Education, 43*(2), 206-219.
- Khanna, Neeta (1993). A Study of the Value Patterns of Students Studying in Teacher Training and General Streams in a Denominational Institute. *Journal of Educational Research and Extension, 30*(2).
- Kishore, L. (2000). Incorporating Value Education in Science Teaching. *School Science, 38*(1), 92-96.
- Kluckhohn, C. F. (1959). *The Scientific Study of Values.* Toronto: University of Toronto Press.

- Kluckhohn, C. F. (1960). *Values in Different Societies, Culture and Behaviours.* Free Press, New York.
- Kothari, C. R. (1985). *Research Methodology: Methods and Techniques.* New Age International Publishers, New Delhi.
- Koul, Lokesh (1997). *Methodology of Educational Research* (10th Revised and Enlarged Edition). Vikash Publishing House Pvt. Ltd., Noida, UP.
- Kruezer, B. Katherine (1992). Women and Leadership: The Effect of Gender, Gender Role Orientation, Socio-Economic Status and Parental Influence on Women's Aspirations to Leader Roles. *Dissertation Abstracts International*, *53*(12), 4495-A.
- Kuppuswamy, B. (1961). *Social Psychology.* Asian Publishing House, Bombay.
- Lin, Meng-Jie (2011). Women's Aspirations for Graduate Education in Taiwan. *International Journal of Educational Development*, *31*(5), 517.
- Lishore, L. (1990). *Value-oriented Education: Foundations and Frontiers-World Overview*. Doaba House, Delhi.
- Macneil, Jerry B. (1900). Study of Life Roles and Values of Senior Undergraduate Education Students. *Dissertation Abstracts International,53*(1), 36-A.
- Maddy, D. J. (1992). Women who shattered the Glass-Ceilings: Post-positivist Inquiry into the Aspirations, Values, Motives and Actions of Women Serving as CEO's of Cooperative Extension Systems. *Dissertation Abstracts International*, *53* (11), 4107-A.
- Manav, Ram Niwas (1981). *A Study of attitudes, Self-concept and Values of Professional and Non-professional College Students and Relationship of these Variables with their Achievement* (Unpublished Ph. D. Thesis). Meerut University, Meerut.
- Mangal, S. K. (2010). *Statistics in Psychology and Education* (Second Edition). PHI Learning Pvt. Ltd., New Delhi.
- Mathur, S. S. (1965). *A Sociological Approach to Indian Education.* Binod Pustak Mandir, Agra.
- Mendoza, Mariateresa Roghi (1991). The Relationship between School Culture and Students' Self-concept, Academic Achievement

and Academic Aspirations in Catholic Secondary Schools as Perceived by Students, faculty/Staff and Parents. *Dissertation Abstracts International*, *52*, 2884-A.

- Menell, Cindy Jo (1991). An Exploration of the Values of Female Counselling Psychology Doctoral Students. *Dissertation Abstracts International, 52,*(12), 306-A.
- Mishra, A. N. (1993). Ways to Inculcate Values in Students. *The Educational Review.*
- Morril, Richard L. (1980). *Teaching Values in College.* Jossey-Bass Publishers, San Francisco, Washington.
- Morris, R. T. (1957). A Typology of Norms. *American Social Review, 21*(13), 610-613.
- Mukherjee, S. K. (2007). *Philosophy and Science of Value Education in the context of Modern India.* Ramakrishna Mission Institute of Culture, Kolkata.
- Musek, Janek (1998). Political and Religious Adherence in relation to Individual Values. *Studia Psychologiea*, *40*(1), 32-59.
- Narayan Karan Reddy, V. (1979). *Man, Education and Values.* B.R. Publishing Corporation, New Delhi.
- Narayanan, S., Shantha, K. D. K., Rao, K. S., and Kumar, K. G. (1994). Value Orientation among Indian and Singapore Business Students. *Indian Journal of Psychology, 69*(3&4), 105-116.
- Nataša, Pantiæ and Theo, Wubbels (2012). The Role of Teachers in inculcating Moral Values: Operationalisation of Concepts. *Journal of Beliefs & Values: Studies in Religion & Education,33*(1), 55-69. Retrieved from http://www.tandfonline.com/doi/full/10.1080/13617672.2012.650030#preview
- NCERT. (1992-98). *Fifth Survey in Educatonal Research.* NCERT, New Delhi.
- NCERT. (1999). *Sixth All India Education Survey.* NCERT, New Delhi.
- NCERT. (2001). *Indian Educational Abstracts 1(1).* NCERT, New Delhi.
- NCERT. (2005). *Journal of Value Education.* January and July-2005, NCERT, New Delhi.

- NCERT. (2006). *Indian Educational Abstracts, 6*(2), NCERT, New Delhi.
- Ojha, R. K., and Bhargava, M. *Mannual for Study of Values Test (SVT).* National Psychological Corporation, Agra-04.
- Padmanaban, T. A. (1992). *Study of the Values of High School Pupils in relation to Certain Selected Variables* (Unpublished Ph. D. Thesis). Annamalai University.
- Pakeeza, S. and Chishti (2012). Role of Religion in Understanding Norms and Values. *International Journal of Asian Social Science, 2*(10), 1851-1857.
- Pamei, Shaganglung (2002). *A Study of Social Motives, Values and Level of Aspiration as Related to Identity Crisis among Naga Students* (Unpublished Ph. D. Thesis). Panjab University, Chandigarh.
- Passi, B. K. and Singh P. (2004). *Value Education.* National Psychological Corporation, Agra.
- Pathak, M. (2002). *A Study of Family Environment, Locus of Control and Level of Aspiration as Predictors of Achievement Motivation among Undergraduate Students* (Unpublished Ph. D, Thesis). Kumaun University, Nainital.
- Pathak, R. D., and Tripathi, S. K. (1998). Information technology and value based education. *University News, 36*(29), 1-7.
- Pradhan, G. C. (1992). Values among Secondary School Students in relation to Moral Judgement, Socio-Economic Status and Sex. *Journal of Educational Research and Extension, 29*(3), 118-126.
- Pradhan, G. C. (1997). Moral Values of School Students in relation to different Personal Values. *Indian Educational Abstract, 3*(37).
- Pradhan, N. N., and Panda, A. K. (1997). Moral Judgement of Tribal Secondary school children in relation to their Sex. *Indian Psychological Abstracts and Reviews,* 4(2), 271.
- Prahallada, N. N. (2000). Contemporary Significance of Value Education. *Value Education in India— Selections from University News-7.* Association of Indian Universities, New Delhi.
- Rajkumari, Sumati (2011). *Impact of Home and School Environments on Values of Adolescent Girls : A Cross-Cultural*

Study (Unpublished Ph. D. Thesis). Avinashilingam Institute for Home Science and Higher Education for Women, Coimbatore.

- Ranu, Sarbjit Kaur (1995). *Value Dimensions of Post-Graduate Students in Relation to their Level of Aspiration and Intelligence* (Unpublished Ph. D Thesis). Punjabi University, Patiala.
- Rao, G. B., Reddy, K. S., and Samiuliah, S. (1997). Behaviour Activity Profiles and Work Values of Employees. *Indian Psychological Abstracts and Reviews, 4*(1), 113.
- Ravindranathan, M. N. (1997). A Study of the Attitude of the Primary School Teachers of Udupi town towards Educational, Economic and Religious aspects of Life. *The Progress of Education, 25*(3), 111-118.
- Rogers, Mary E. (2010). A Multivariate Analysis of Personality, Values and Expectations as Correlates of Career Aspirations of Final year Medical Students. *International Journal for Educational and Vocational Guidance, 10*(3), 177-189.
- Ruhela, S. P. (ed.). (1986). *Human Values and Education*. Sterling Publishers Pvt. Ltd., New Delhi.
- Russel, Betrand (1967). *Impact of Science in Society*. George Allen and Unwin Ltd., London.
- Sahoo, K. C., Biswal, A. and Khandai, H. (1998). Student's Perceptions of Present Secular Values. *The Progress of Education, 69*(9), 184-186.
- Saraswathi, T. S. (ed.). (1999). *Culture, Socialisation and Human Development: Theory, Research and Applications in India*. Sage Publications, New Delhi.
- Sati, B. D. (1991). *Comparative Study of Needs, Values, Aspirations and Adjustments in relation to Academic Achievement of Scheduled Caste and other Students of Secondary Schools of Kumaun* (Unpublished Ph. D. Thesis). Kumaun University, Nainital.
- Schludermann, E. H., Schludermann, S. M., and Cam-Loi (2000). Religiosity, Prosocial Values, and Adjustment among Students in Catholic High Schools in Canada. *Journal of Beliefs & Values: Studies in Religion & Education, 21*(1), 99-115. Retrieved from http://www.tandfonline.com/doi/abs/10.1080/13617670050002363

- Schoon, I. (2006). *Risk and Resilience: Adaptations in Changing Times*. Cambridge University Press, Cambridge.
- Shagufta, M. and A., Mariya (2012). Contribution of Value Education towards Human Development in India: Theoretical Concepts. *International Journal of Asian Social Science 2*(12), 2283-2290.
- Shah, H. M. (1992). *An Investigation into the Values of the Higher Secondary School Students of Saurashtra* (Unpublished Ph. D. Thesis). Saurashtra University.
- Sharma, N. P. (1997). Can Values be Taught? *Shiksha Bharati, 2*(2), 32-34.
- Shivamurti, M., Ansari, M. R., and Venkataranganaika, K. (1992). Study in Value Orientation, Knowledge and Adoption Behaviour of Sericulturists in Dharwad District, Karnataka. *Asian Journal of Psychology and Education,25*.
- Shrimali, K. L. (1971). *A Search for Values in Indian Education*. Vikash Publications, Delhi.
- Simpson, Km. K. (2007). *Socio-Genetic Needs, Level of Aspiration and Self-Concept as Predictors of Risk-taking Behaviour among Adolescents* (Unpublished Ph. D. Thesis). Kumaun University, Nainital.
- Singh, A. K., and Gupta, Alpana Sen (1997). Some personality Determinants of Value and Intelligence. *Indian Journal of Psychometry and Education, 27*(2), 111-114. In *Indian Educational Abstracts, 1*(1).
- Singh, Iqbal (1993). *A Study of Value Dimensions of Secondary School Teachers in relation to their Sex, Age and Experience* (Unpublished M. Phil. Dissertation). Punjabi University, Patiala.
- Singh, R. P. (1997). A Study of Values of Urban and Rural Adolescent Students. *Praachi Journal of Psychocultural Dimensions, 9*(1), 7-11.
- Singh, T., and Pathak, S. (1997). Human Environment Relationships: An Empirical study of Attitudes, Values and Perceptions. *Indian Psychological Abstracts and Reviews, 4*(1),90.

- Smulders, A. E. M. (1995). Perception of Private Companies in Malaysia on Value Education. *Perspectives in Education, 11*(2), 109-117. In *Indian Educational Abstracts, 1*(1).
- Sprenger, Edward (1928). *Type of Men*. New York, Skehart.
- Strand, Steve and Winston, Joe (2008). *Educational Aspirations in Inner City Schools. Educational Studies*, *34*(4), 249-267.
- Sucharitha, R. (2012). *A Study of Moral Judgement of Secondary School Students in Relation to Some Variables* (Unpublished Ph. D. Thesis). Sri Padmavati Mahila Visva Vidyalayam, Tirupati, India.
- Taj, Haseen and Rekha, S. (1995). National Integration through Value Oriented Activities. *Psycho-Linqua*, *25*(182), 73-78.
- Tripathi, Sujit Ram (2008). *Patterns of Social Identity and Value Orientation and their Implication for Conflict Resolution* (Unpublished Ph. D. Thesis). University of Delhi, Delhi.
- Vaithilingam, M. (1999). *Aspirations, Value of Children and Fertility behaviour in Rural Tamil Nadu* (Unpublished Ph. D. Thesis). International Institute for Population Sciences, (Deemed University), DEONAR, Mumbai.
- Venkataiah, N. (ed.). (1998). *Value Education*, APH Publishing Corporation, New Delhi.
- Verma, D. (1996). A study of Value Pattern among College Youth of Rohilkhand region with special reference to Sense of Responsibility. *Indian Educational Abstract, 1,* 40.
- Verma, V. P., Das, Rajalakshmi and Swain, C. Bimal (1993). Values of Adolescent Students as a Function of their Sex and Rural Urban Inhabitation. *Indian Educational Review, January 1993*, 71- 79.
- Vijayalakshmi, Ghali (2006). Prioritisation of Secondary School Children's Values by their Parents and Teacher. *Educational Tracks*, *6*(7), 34-37.
- Wadhwa, B. S. (2010). *Research and Statistics in Education.* Tweenty First Century Publications, Patiala.
- Wilgenbusch, T. and Merrell, K. W. (1999). Gender Differences in Self-Concept among Children and Adolescents: A Meta-Analysis of Multidimensional Studies. *School Psychology Quarterly, 14*, 101-120.

Index